**Presented
to the
Bowling Green State University
Libraries and Learning Resources**

Donated by:

Dillon Press &

Cooperative Services for

Children's Literature

Margaret Sanger

"Every Child a Wanted Child"

Margaret Sanger

"Every Child a Wanted Child"

by Nancy Whitelaw

A People in Focus Book

DILLON PRESS
New York

Maxwell Macmillan Canada
Toronto

Maxwell Macmillan International
New York   Oxford   Singapore   Sydney

To Eva Whitelaw Barrett, my granddaughter—with love

Acknowledgments

The author is grateful to Peter C. Engelman, assistant editor, Sophia Smith Collection, who read the manuscript, offered many valuable suggestions, and helped collect and label the photos. She thanks him also for his strong support and encouragement.

Funding for this book was made available in part by the Fund for the Arts in Chautauqua County, which is managed by the Arts Council for Chautauqua County.

Library of Congress Cataloging-in-Publication Data

Whitelaw, Nancy.
    Margaret Sanger : "every child a wanted child" / by Nancy Whitelaw. — 1st ed.
    p. cm. — (People in focus)
    Includes bibliographical references (p. 157) and index.
    Summary: A biography of Margaret Sanger, the indomitable fighter for birth control and a feminist who asked women to take responsibility for their freedom.
    ISBN 0-87518-581-9
    1. Sanger, Margaret, 1879-1966–Juvenile literature. 2. Feminists–United States–Biography–Juvenile literature. 3. Birth control–United States–History–Juvenile literature. [1. Sanger, Margaret, 1879-1966. 2. Feminists. 3. Birth control–History.] I. Title. II. Series.
HQ764.S3.W6   1994
305.42'092—dc20
[B]   93-13635

Copyright © 1994 by Nancy Whitelaw

All rights reserved. No part of this book may be reproduced or transmitted in any form or by any means, electronic or mechanical, including photocopying, recording, or by any information storage and retrieval system, without permission in writing from the Publisher.

Dillon Press	Maxwell Macmillan Canada, Inc.
Macmillan Publishing Company	1200 Eglinton Avenue East
866 Third Avenue	Suite 200
New York, NY 10022	Don Mills, Ontario M3C 3N1

Macmillan Publishing Company is part of the Maxwell Communication Group of Companies.

First edition

Printed in the United States of America

10 9 8 7 6 5 4 3 2 1

Contents

Introduction		7
Chapter One	From Maggie Higgins to Margaret Sanger	11
Chapter Two	"I Would Tell the World"	27
Chapter Three	The *Woman Rebel*	41
Chapter Four	Back to America, Back to Court	55
Chapter Five	The Brownsville Clinic Opens and Closes	68
Chapter Six	A Major Victory	86
Chapter Seven	A Question of Freedom of Speech	97
Chapter Eight	A New Clinic, A New Husband	107
Chapter Nine	A Raid on the Research Bureau	119
Chapter Ten	Committee on Federal Legislation	129
Chapter Eleven	A Better World	139
Appendix One	A Glossary of Special Terms	153
Appendix Two	Margaret Sanger: A Time Line	155
Selected Bibliography		157
Index		159

Introduction

Eight-year-old Maggie Higgins took one last look at her feet as she stepped on the first tie of the narrow railroad bridge.

This was in Corning, New York, in 1887. Maggie was working on her plan to become brave.

"Now don't look down again," she told herself. "Walk across this bridge with your head up high. Don't think about the river swishing over the rocks. Don't think about a train coming the other way. Think about making yourself strong."

She planted her right foot firmly on the wooden tie. "Eyes straight ahead. Look at the farms on the other side of the river." She lifted her left foot and sent it searching over empty space for the next tie. Left foot down. Right foot up and searching. Right foot down.

Left foot. Right foot. Left foot. "Stronger. Stronger. Every step, stronger."

She guessed she was about halfway across.

Right foot. Left foot. Right . . .

Quietly, then louder and louder, the rails began to hum. Suddenly the hum was drowned out by the shriek of a train whistle. She looked over her shoulder. A huge black locomotive was heading straight for her.

Maggie fell on one knee as the bridge shook with the weight of the iron monster. She knew she had to make her body as flat as possible. She let her feet and legs slip down between the ties as she grabbed for the edge of the tie in front of her. Her fingers curled around the rough edge with all her strength.

Her eardrums ached with the clattering and screeching of steel wheels on iron rails. She winced as hot cinders flew at her arms and face and back.

The next thing she knew, a man's arm was around her waist, pulling her upward. Strong fingers forced her to release her grasp on the tie. She was lifted to her feet where she wobbled and swayed, trying to get her balance. Her rescuer, a friend of her father's, steadied her. He had been fishing, he said, when he saw her do this dangerous thing. He scolded her, gave her a little spank, and told her to go right back home.

Maggie waited until he was out of sight. Then she turned around and finished her trip across the bridge.

Another fear beaten! Earlier that year, Maggie had promised herself to get rid of her fears. Before that, she sang when she went down into the cellar, hoping to scare away strange beings who lurked there. No more! Now Maggie walked down the stairs without a sound. She used to take a candle when she went upstairs to bed, swinging the flame to force monsters into hiding. No more! Now Maggie went to her bedroom in the dark. She used to be ashamed of her fear of the railroad bridge. Now even that fear could not stop her. She was free to go over the bridge whenever she wanted to.

Later in life, Maggie Louisa Higgins (Sanger) would dedicate her life to helping women to overcome their fears and to accept the responsibilities that freedom brings.

She was born in the late 1800s, when most women accepted a passive role. For centuries women had obeyed their parents, their church leaders, their government officials, their doctors, and their husbands. They had been afraid to take responsibility for their own bodies, their families, and their futures.

Margaret Sanger showed them the way to freedom from fear. For this, she was scorned, ridiculed, and humiliated. She was arrested, and she was sent to prison. Still, she never wavered in her determination to bring reliable and accessible birth control to any woman who wanted it.

After more than 50 years of struggle, Margaret saw much of her dream fulfilled. Because of her, women all over the world are challenged to take responsibility for their lives and to participate in making this a better world for all families.

Chapter One

From Maggie Higgins to Margaret Sanger

1879-1902

During this time . . .
- ❖Mark Twain wrote *Huckleberry Finn*.
- ❖The first bicycles were manufactured in America.
- ❖Basketball was invented by J. Naismith.
- ❖A carriage driver was arrested for speeding at 12 m.p.h.
- ❖Ball-bearing roller skates were patented.

Maggie, born in Corning, New York, in 1879, was the sixth child in a family of eleven children. She could always find a few brothers or sisters to take parts in the plays she loved to put on.

Life was busy for the Higgins children. Each day they walked the five miles to school and back. The boys

Maggie at 14

took care of the cows and chickens; the girls helped with housework and younger children. They all played baseball, skated, swam, and hunted together in the little free time that they had.

Maggie created a picture of herself. "I realized I was made up of two Me's," she said. One was the Thinking Maggie, who acted slowly and thoughtfully. It was the Thinking Maggie who made up rules for overcoming her fears. The other was the Emotional Maggie, who acted and talked without thinking. It was the Emotional Maggie who continued her trip across the railroad bridge when told to go home.

Maggie's father was Michael Higgins, a stone mason who made decorations for gravestones. Maggie sometimes watched him at work—rounding out an angel's mouth, chipping away stone around the wings, carving the strong, straight lines of a cross.

Mr. Higgins loved to talk and to argue. He'd spend hours in a tavern, on a street corner, or anywhere people would listen to him. He urged his children to talk, question, and argue just as he did. From him, Maggie learned to criticize government, laws, the church, customs, and traditions.

"Don't be afraid to speak your mind," Maggie's father would say. "Always say what you mean."

From the time she was a little girl, Maggie heard

Michael Higgins, Maggie's father, a stonecutter

lots of criticisms and complaints, lots of strong opinions and arguing. Mr. Higgins disagreed with the way America was run. Like other Socialists, he believed that government should take control of business and industry.

Mr. Higgins had rebellious ideas about women, too. At that time, most people believed that a woman's role in life was to be a wife and mother. Mr. Higgins accepted the traditional role for his own wife. He was content to have her bear 11 children, even though each pregnancy created serious health problems for her. However, he believed that his daughters might be educated to accept responsibilities and challenges just as his sons were. He told Maggie and the other children, "Leave the world better because you, my child, have dwelt in it."

Mr. Higgins praised Susan B. Anthony, who was fighting for women's suffrage, the right to vote. He even said that women should be allowed to wear trousers if they wanted to!

Maggie's mother, Anne Higgins, did not have the time or the strength for these ideas. Shortly after her marriage, Mrs. Higgins contracted tuberculosis. She was pregnant 18 times in her 30 years of marriage. She gave birth to 11 living children.

Young Maggie did not know that each pregnancy made her mother's tuberculosis more severe. All the little girl knew was that her mother, a frail and sober woman, frequently coughed and gasped for breath, leaning against walls and furniture for support. Maggie lived with a constant fear that her mother would die during one of these spasms.

Maggie's family did not have much money. Mr. Higgins might have made more money if he had not argued so much. When he argued against religious teachings, some potential customers decided to have their gravestones decorated by someone else. When he argued against the government, other potential customers did the same. His drinking problem made matters worse.

Sometimes Maggie was able to talk easily about the family finances. Once she said that the Higginses lived the life of a typical artist's family: "Chicken one day, feathers the next." She always remembered an incident that occurred because some of the Higgins children had only one set of clothes. When one of the boys ripped his trousers, he had to wear his sister's clothes while his mother mended his only pair of pants.

But the bad times, as when her mother had to take in washing to make extra money, also left a strong impression on Maggie. She watched her father fight for one losing cause after another, and she saw the financial problems these struggles caused. Like her father she became a reformer. Unlike her father, she tried to avoid situations in which she might lose more than she would gain.

The Higginses were not the poorest family in Corning. Hundreds of families lived in small houses close to the Chemung River. Their children swarmed over the area, fighting for playing space on tiny plots of land. Wealthy families, owners and managers of the factories and railroads, lived in large homes above the belching smoke of the factory chimneys. Their children roamed all over the hillside with lots of room to play in. Maggie learned at an early age about the different living standards between wealthy people and poor people.

Growing up in a large family gave Maggie an important advantage. She learned to fight for her rights, even in school where girls were supposed to be especially quiet. When she was in the eighth grade, Maggie received a luxurious gift—a pair of warm gloves. She was so pleased that she wore them in school.

The teacher reacted. "Miss Higgins, you are so busy admiring your gloves you seem to be above a little thing like paying attention."

Her classmates laughed.

Maggie ran out of the room. At home, she announced, "I am never going back to that school again!"

At first, her family thought she was just being dramatic again. But the Emotional Maggie would not budge.

"I'll go to jail! I'll work, I'll starve, I'll die! But back to that school and teacher, I will never go!"

The family soon realized that Maggie would not change her mind. Since education was important to them, they searched for another school for her. They found a boarding school, Claverack College (a secondary school, not a college), near Hudson, New York. Claverack advertised that it taught the elements of a "pure and noble womanhood." The school made special arrangements for students who could not pay the full tuition. The rest of the fees would be made up by Maggie's two sisters who worked as mothers' helpers and by Maggie's work in the school dining room.

In 1896, when she entered Claverack, Maggie became known as Margaret. She took courses in public speaking, painting, and literature. Perhaps she did not know it, but she had become a beautiful young lady. Her brown hair sparkled with red highlights, her figure was small and well proportioned, and her violet-gray eyes attracted attention. Margaret found herself at home with a group of young women who loved to argue and to rebel. They often complained about their lack of freedom to come and go as they pleased.

At one point, Margaret decided that she wanted to become an actress. She wrote to a casting agency in New York City. They replied with a request for a photo and a list of her measurements. Margaret dropped the idea.

Dating was forbidden, of course. However, Margaret and her friends sometimes found spots where they could meet secretly with boys from a nearby school.

One night she and her friends sneaked off campus

to a dance hall. They had a fine time until the principal appeared!

She told about this incident in her autobiography. The principal said that she was a ringleader. "You must make your choice," he warned, "whether to get yourself and others into difficulty, or else guide yourself and others into constructive activities which will do you and them credit." Margaret never forgot that lecture.

She had a problem with her public speaking course. The very thought of talking in front of a class left her with a trembling voice and a nervous stomach. She made up a plan to overcome the fear, just as she had made plans to overcome her fears of the cellar, her dark bedroom, and the railroad bridge. As she described it in her autobiography, her plan began and ended in the cemetery:

> I studied and wrote as never before, stealing away to the cemetery and standing on the monuments over the graves. Each day in the quiet of the dead, I repeated and repeated that speech out loud.

By the end of the term, she had enough courage to speak on a controversial topic, women's rights. She also had enough courage to star in several plays.

Margaret had to leave Claverack before her final year because her sisters could not continue to help her

Margaret at 16, posing for a photo at Claverack College with an admirer

financially. No longer a student, she was expected to marry. Margaret was not interested in marriage.

Young women who did not marry had three kinds of jobs open to them—typing, teaching, and nursing. Margaret had no interest in typing. She decided to teach. After six months teaching English to immigrant children in New Jersey, she came back to Corning to nurse her dying mother.

While the family watched helplessly, Mrs. Higgins spit up blood every time she coughed. She grew weaker until she was unable to walk at all. In the spring of 1899, she died.

At first, Margaret thought that she would stay in Corning to take her mother's place as head of the household. But she soon grew tired of keeping house for her father and the younger children. She was bored with scrubbing, mending, ironing, and worrying about money for food. Besides, she didn't like living in Corning. The family house and the town brought back memories of her exhausted mother. It was time for 20-year-old Margaret Higgins to leave home.

She might have thought more intensely about becoming a doctor, but she could not afford the years of study. Her next choice was nursing. She enrolled in a nursing school near White Plains, New York. As a student nurse, she received board, room, and a

Anne Purcell Higgins, Margaret's mother

small salary in return for her work in the hospital. Wearing her candy-striped uniform, she emptied bedpans, changed beds, and cleaned. She also brought in water, pitcher by pitcher, from an outdoor well. When she became sick and exhausted, doctors found a touch of tuberculosis in her adrenal glands. The illness lingered, but Margaret continued her studies.

Childbirth had always fascinated her. She had watched the births of some of her sisters and brothers. Now as a nurse who could help mothers, she was even more fascinated.

Sometimes she attended patients who lived miles away from the hospital. While she waited for the doctor, she started boiling the water, usually over a wood stove in the kitchen. When the doctor arrived, she was ready to sterilize his instruments. Often, the doctor arrived too late for the delivery. When this happened, Margaret delivered the baby herself.

Sometimes mothers confided in Margaret that they hoped this would be the last baby for a while. She sympathized with mothers who made comments like:

> *"I want to let this baby have all my attention for a while, at least."*

> *"I have had four babies and 3 miscarriages in the*

Margaret, student nurse

past ten years. I don't have the strength for another pregnancy."

"My husband only works part-time. We have seven children now. We can't afford another one."

Some mothers asked Margaret how they could stop having children—at least for a while. Margaret suggested that they ask their doctors, who had much more knowledge and experience than she did. Once she told a doctor that a woman had asked her this question. The doctor was furious. How could a patient talk about such a matter with a young student nurse! He didn't want any patients to ask him about it, either. He would take care of problems as he knew best, and he did not want any interference from women.

When she was 23 years old, Margaret met 28-year old Bill Sanger, a tall, dark, and handsome architect. Sanger was immediately obsessed with this slim and pretty redhead. For weeks, he courted her with expensive dinner dates, daily bouquets of flowers, and long love notes. He wrote about wanting to build a home for her "with you as Presiding Queen, dearest." This courtship appealed to Margaret's love of the dramatic. The Emotional Margaret agreed to marry him. The Thinking Margaret added that she would prefer to finish her nursing degree first.

One afternoon in August 1902, Bill picked her up for an afternoon date. They rode around in a horse and buggy for a couple of hours, arguing. Bill wanted to marry right away. Margaret wanted to get her degree. School rules prohibited married students.

Suddenly, Bill stopped the carriage at the home of a minister. He showed her a marriage license and said that the minister was expecting them.

Angry, confused—and in love—Margaret took part in the ceremony. After a quick wedding kiss, the new Mrs. William Sanger had to rush back to the hospital for her late afternoon shift.

Margaret's head spun with questions as she bathed and fed patients, made beds, and cleaned wards. Why had she allowed Bill to dominate? Did she want to be Mrs. William Sanger? Should she leave school right away? Should she pretend that nothing was different until she graduated?

She wrote to her sister Nan:

Here I am no longer a Higgins. That man of mine simply carried me off. I vow I will not live with such a beast of a man.

But in the same letter, she showed her confusion:

He is so happy and so am I . . . I am sure I could not have a better husband—he is my ideal in many ways but I wanted to wait.

A couple of weeks after the ceremony, Margaret made a dramatic decision. She quit nursing. She and Bill settled into an apartment on 119th Street in Manhattan.

Chapter Two

"I Would Tell the World"

1902-1912

During this time . . .
- ❖Orville Wright flew a plane at 30 m.p.h.
- ❖A subway system opened in New York City.
- ❖The ice cream cone was "invented."
- ❖The Girl Scouts and Boy Scouts were organized.
- ❖Zippers came into use.

Margaret and Bill were delighted when she became pregnant. But soon she felt weak. The pregnancy brought back the tuberculosis. With agonizing memories of her mother's health problems, Margaret listened to the doctor. He prescribed weeks of rest at a sanatorium in the Adirondack Mountains of New

York, where she could receive constant care.

At the sanatorium, she was encouraged to spend as much time as possible outside. She spent hours on a porch, wrapped in heavy blankets, no matter what the weather. She was advised to do as little as possible. Exercising, even walking, was frowned on. Margaret lay around all day, trying to force down huge meals, missing her family and friends, and watching other patients cough up blood and pus into little tin cups. She was fearful, lonely, and terribly bored.

Stuart Sanger, a healthy baby, was born in November 1903. Margaret still suffered from tuberculosis. The doctor again prescribed lots of rest and fresh air. Margaret and Stuart moved to a farmhouse near the sanatorium. They spent months there. She tried to eat the prescribed daily diet of a dozen eggs, four quarts of milk, meat, vegetables, and medicine.

Soon Margaret became depressed. Physically weak and emotionally discouraged, she lost interest in life. Bill and other members of her family despaired. Finally, a doctor at the sanatorium reached through Margaret's desolation.

"Do something. Want something," he told her.

These words gave Margaret the courage to believe that she could control herself and her life again. What she wanted to do was to leave the clinic! So, against doctors' orders, she and Stuart returned to Bill. Happy to be home again, she slowly regained her strength.

She and Bill and Stuart settled in a newly developed community of young families. Margaret soon became dissatisfied with housekeeping routines. Bill began working on plans for their dream house. An elegant white stucco house—called a showplace by the local newspaper—it was built in Hastings-on-Hudson. The Sangers moved into their new home on a cold and blustery day in February 1908.

A few nights later, they went to bed after stoking the coal furnace high. They awakened when the maid yelled, "Fire!" Soon their dream house was in flames.

They escaped with their lives, and they found temporary housing. Margaret was shocked to discover that they faced serious financial trouble. She believed that Bill had betrayed her by not informing her of the debt created by the purchase of the land and construction of the house. Later she said that the experience had shown her that material possessions cannot bring happiness.

Almost immediately, Bill began working to restore the house. The next summer, they moved back into their home. For some time, Margaret complained that the house was not the same as before. She said that it smelled of smoke and charred wood.

Grant was born in the summer of 1908. Peggy came in 1910. Margaret was busier than ever, but she was no happier. Although she loved her children, she did not like the work that came with them.

When Peggy was only a few months old, she came down with polio, an acute viral disease, and was left with one leg shorter than the other. Despite her nurse's training, Margaret neglected her infant daughter's special needs until about a year later, when Bill insisted that the child be fitted for a brace.

Margaret forgot about mealtimes, fastened torn clothing with safety pins, and ignored daily cleaning tasks. Her interest in nursing saved her from complete boredom. When Margaret heard that a neighbor youngster had fallen or that a baby was bothered by a constant cough or fever, she rushed to help. The challenge of nursing filled a deep need for Margaret.

But the nursing was not enough. Margaret was bored with the neighborhood talk of family budgets, clothes, and recipes. Like her father, Margaret craved the excitement of a city where she could meet people who were active outside the home. She wanted to talk and argue about politics, world affairs, and social conditions.

Bill felt the same way about life in the suburbs. Margaret confided later in her autobiography that they

William Sanger, Margaret's husband

were both "feeling what amounted to a world hunger, the pull and haul towards wider horizons."

Like Margaret's father, Bill Sanger found saving money difficult. They did not recover financially from the fire. Finally in 1910, Bill sold the property because he needed cash desperately.

They moved to an apartment on West 135th Street in New York City. Bill's mother moved in with them. For the first time in several years, Margaret was free from household duties.

New York City was an exciting place in the early 1900s. Change was in the air. Everywhere people were asking: What can we do to make life better?

Some wanted to make life better for themselves. These included wealthy people like John Jacob Astor, who built a home on Fifth Avenue complete with a ballroom that held 400 guests. The back of one of Mrs. Astor's hostess gowns was so thickly encrusted with diamonds that she could not relax in her chair.

Some wanted to make life better for others. They wanted to help the thousands of poor New York workers and their families. Journalist Jacob Riis, who became well known for his photos of poverty-stricken immigrants, described their living conditions: "crazy buildings, leaking garrets, crowded filthy tenements in rear yards . . . scarcely fit to shelter brutes."

Workers demonstrated and went on strike for better working conditions. Reporters exposed landlords who rented filthy and unsafe tenements. Socialists argued that the government should control essential business and industry. Capitalists argued that the government should stay out of business. Communists argued that workers should seize control of the government. Anarchists argued that there should be no government at all. Eugenicists demanded laws to prohibit child-bearing by couples whom they classified as physically, mentally, or emotionally inferior.

Bill was a Socialist, and Margaret was pleased to join him at Party meetings. Like her father, she was eager to state her opinion and to take sides in an argument. She loved the drama of passionate speeches and the audience response. She met and admired people who had been jailed for demonstrating, sometimes violently, against what they considered injustice. Margaret herself was arrested twice for helping strikers.

Emma Goldman, an anarchist, was one of these people. She co-authored a pamphlet, *Why and How the Poor Should Not Have Many Children*, describing the use of birth control devices. She described condoms, devices worn by males to prevent sperm from reaching the egg, and diaphragms, devices worn by females for the same purpose. She wrote in a pamphlet that poor children "glut the labor market, tend to lower wages, and are a menace to the welfare of the working class." Goldman was jailed for 60 days for distributing these pamphlets through the mail, a violation of law.

As a nurse, Margaret was interested in Goldman's views on birth control. Margaret was convinced that frequent pregnancies created health problems for both mothers and babies. Statistics showed that about 200 babies died for every 1,000 births.

Margaret sent out word that she was available to help with childbirth. Soon she had more calls than she could handle. Most of her patients were poor people who lived in tenements. These apartment buildings had been built cheaply and quickly to house the thousands of immigrants who came to New York City looking for work. Often two and three families crowded into a three-room apartment. Many apartments had no windows. In a typical arrangement, six or eight families living on two floors might share a single toilet. The children's playground was the street, the same place where residents dumped their garbage.

Day after day Margaret climbed up flights of dark stairs, surrounded by smells of boiled onions and fried fish, garbage and trash, rot and decay. Most of the women Margaret attended did not have the time, the strength, or the money to care for several children. Over

Tenements in New York City, early 1900s

and over again, women asked her: "What can I do to stop another baby? Please help me."

Margaret did not know what to say. Researchers believe that she and Bill had access to diaphragms. But these devices require fitting by a doctor, a service that was too expensive for wives of common laborers. Some women bought birth control products from mail-order houses and drug stores: pessaries, devices like diaphragms; suppositories, medications inserted in the vagina to destroy sperm; and douches, devices to flush sperm from the vagina. Although these products were illegal, customers who could pay for them could obtain them. Margaret knew that the women whom she attended could not pay for them.

Margaret did tell women about a less expensive device, the condom. Men commonly used condoms to protect themselves from diseases when they engaged in intercourse with prostitutes. These devices put the responsibility for contraception on the male. When Margaret described them, the women shook their heads. Some husbands did not care; others would forget. Besides, condoms were associated with prostitution. Wives would not mention such a device to their husbands.

Some 40 years earlier, the mailing of materials about contraception had been declared illegal. The lawmakers said that these materials were "obscene," "lewd," and "lascivious." In that year, Anthony Comstock was a lobbyist for the Young Men's Christian Association and, largely because of his campaign, the legislation became known as the Comstock Laws.

This attitude toward contraception started a movement that spread beyond federal regulation of mail. Many states made laws restricting publication and circulation of material related to contraception.

Most doctors supported the Comstock Laws. They believed that information about contraception should not be made public. They said that sex was a personal matter, and only indecent people would discuss it. These doctors, mostly male, also believed that women should not be allowed to make important decisions, especially in matters like family planning.

Margaret's patients—poor, desperate, and without access to contraceptives—often chose abortion as a way to limit their family size. Among these unfortunate women, one out of every five pregnancies was aborted, according to authorities at the time. Often, the women could not afford reliable medical assistance and went to so-called doctors who used unsafe procedures. Worse, some women who could afford no help at all injured themselves seriously while trying to abort with a knitting needle or other sharp instrument.

At the time, Margaret did not know how to make her concerns known to the public. Then the editor of the *Call*, a Socialist newspaper, contacted Margaret.

"Our speaker for a woman's group is unable to come. Will you take her place?"

"I can't speak."

"You simply have to."

So Margaret went to the room where an audience of ten women waited. She tried not to think about her trembling voice and nervous stomach. She thought about what she wanted to tell these women. She remembered what she had learned in public speaking and drama classes. Once she began to talk, her message rang out loud and clear. The message was that every worker and his family need and deserve good health.

The women were intrigued by this vibrant young woman with the reddish brown curls. She caught their attention with her enthusiasm. They asked question after question about how to improve family health. And they asked her to speak again. Word about Margaret's talk sped through the community. Seventy-five women showed up at the second meeting. The editor of the *Call* suggested that Margaret could reach a larger audience by writing for the newspaper.

Margaret wrote about the need for contraception. She asked how anyone dared to prevent women from learning about contraception. She believed that every child should be a wanted child. In a dramatic statement in the *Call*, she complained that "[men] were too oversexed, too tainted with the sins of their fathers, to be able to look upon women's claims as their own." She asked why men couldn't see that women cannot possibly give adequate care to families that grow faster than the available time, space, and money.

In her autobiography, Margaret tells a story about Sadie Sachs. The story is that Jake Sachs, a truck driver, called Margaret one night. Sadie Sachs, his wife, was critically ill. Sadie, a mother of three, was in her early 20s. She had tried to abort a fourth pregnancy, and had developed blood poisoning from the attempt.

Margaret called a doctor who performed emergency care.

"If you have another baby, there won't be any need to send for me," the doctor told Sadie.

"But what can I do to stop it?" she asked.

"Tell Jake to sleep on the roof," answered the doctor, and he left.

Sadie wept. She asked Margaret what to do. Was there no answer except to give up the normal relationship of husband and wife? Margaret had no answer. She could only nurse Sadie through three difficult weeks of recovery.

A few months later, Jake begged Margaret to come back. Sadie had tried her own method of abortion again. This time she did not survive.

Some researchers doubt the truth of this story. They suspect that Margaret made up Sadie as a representative of hundreds of women in the same situation. Whatever the truth, the problems of married women who could not limit their families affected Margaret deeply. She resolved: "There was only one thing to be done. I would tell the world what was going on in the lives of these poor women. No matter what it should cost, I would be heard."

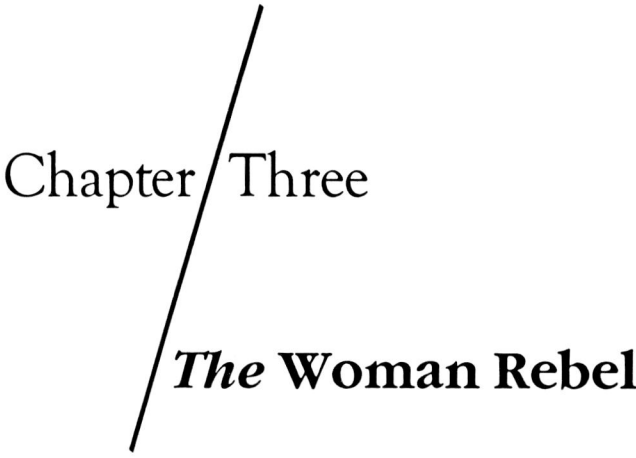

Chapter Three

The Woman Rebel

1912-1914

During this time . . .
- ❖President Woodrow Wilson proclaimed the second Sunday in May as Mother's Day.
- ❖U.S. citizens paid their first federal income taxes.
- ❖Suffragettes were arrested for making public protests.
- ❖Erector sets and Tinkertoys became popular.
- ❖A Model T Ford car could be assembled in 93 minutes.

Margaret became bolder. In November 1912, she began a series of articles for the *Call* entitled "What Every Girl Should Know." Sexual love was "natural, clean and healthful," she wrote. She explained about a woman's body and reproductive cycles. She also cautioned against contagious diseases that could be transmitted during sexual intercourse.

That did it! Post office officials seized the November issue of the *Call*. They declared that under the Comstock Laws it was illegal to mail material about sexually transmitted diseases. Shortly after that, editors of the *Call* published another edition. Under the headline WHAT EVERY GIRL SHOULD KNOW, they left a large blank box. Under the box, they wrote: "*Nothing* by order of the Post Office Department."

Margaret resolved to fight until the Comstock Laws were repealed. She believed that many people would support the cause once they understood how important it was to them.

She appealed to married couples. She said that many infants died soon after birth because their mothers had not been strong enough to nourish them through the pregnancy. Others died later because families could not afford to feed and care for them. She wanted parents to understand that children were insecure in a home where husband and wife could not share physical love because of fear of unlimited family growth. She created a new slogan: "Every child a wanted child." Individually, men and women may have agreed with her. But few couples could break custom and talk freely about sex and reproduction, even to each other.

Margaret asked workers to help. She told them that birth control would eliminate poverty, unemployment, and crime. She said that capitalistic employers wanted women to have more and more children. When these children were old enough to work, they would compete for jobs. The competition would allow employers to offer low wages and poor working conditions. Employees may have agreed with Margaret, but few dared to risk their jobs by agreeing with her publicly.

Margaret wrote to government officials. She asked them to support her to help the economy. She reminded them that large families of poor children result in high welfare costs. She also said that large families had more mentally retarded and physically handicapped children than smaller families. The officials did not want to be involved in this controversial issue.

She hoped that poor people would join her campaign. But members of needy families had only one thought: how to meet their weekly bills for food, clothing, and shelter. They had neither time nor energy to think about a future beyond the next rent payment or medical bill.

She guessed that feminists, who were fighting for equal rights with men, would support birth control. How could women have equal rights with men if they did not have control over their bodies? But most feminists believed that they should focus on equal rights in education, work, and citizenship. They would focus on birth control later.

She argued that Socialists should work with her. She had traveled to New Jersey and Massachusetts to help families of striking workers. Now she appealed for help for her cause, urging Socialists to understand that access to birth control information and devices would help these desperate families. But the Party was dominated by males and, like most other organizations, was sexist. Women and their family problems could not be considered as important as men and their problems in the workplace. Socialist action centered on demonstrations and strikes for better working conditions.

Could Margaret play the role of rebel alone, with no supporting cast? Could she find an audience to listen to her? If they did listen, would they scoff, insult, criticize, and humiliate her? Was she afraid? Could she, or should she, give up? Margaret remembered her father's words: "Leave the world better because you, my child, have dwelt in it." She knew how to make the world better. She had to continue her campaign.

As she considered her role, she realized that the Thinking Margaret was making no progress for her cause. The Emotional Margaret must take dramatic steps to draw attention to the situation. She decided to write the brochure that women were begging for. They wanted specific information about how to prevent unwanted pregnancies. They would get it!

She planned out the next scenes. She would be arrested for sending the brochures through the mail. In a final scene at her trial, she would prove that the Comstock Laws were unconstitutional.

Before she could begin work on this project, she felt that she needed more specific information on birth control practices. In the fall of 1913, she was delighted when Bill suggested that the family go to Paris, where he could study art. He had quit his job at the architectural firm, saying that he would not be a "wage slave." He would spend the mortgage payments from the sale of the Hastings-on-Hudson property in an attempt to make his fortune as an artist in Paris. Margaret would be able to study birth control methods and policies in Europe, where family planning was more advanced. There she would find the information she needed to write a brochure for American women.

In the French capital, Margaret talked to women who took responsibility for their sexuality. These women believed that sex was essential to a loving relationship. It was not an indecent act. Some women controlled family size with diaphragms and pessaries. Some used

Grant, Peggy, and Stuart Sanger in Paris in 1913

sponges, devices inserted in the vagina that prevented conception by changing the chemical balance in the uterus. The sponges also acted as a barrier to sperm. Some used douches, devices to flush semen from the vagina. Margaret collected samples of these items.

By December, she was ready to return to America. She had the specific information she sought. She had stories of women who had some control over their lives. Nothing could stop Margaret now. Not men who demanded control of women and sex. Not women who were ashamed to discuss their bodies. Not the Comstock Laws. Not even her husband, who wanted to stay in Paris. On December 31, Margaret and her children boarded a ship headed for New York.

Bill wrote, supporting her: "Propogate an idea—no matter how revolutionary." But he sent no money, and Margaret had to rely on payments from the Hastings-on-Hudson house for food and shelter.

Once back in Manhattan, she planned to publish an independent monthly newspaper, the *Woman Rebel*, designed ". . . to stimulate working women to think for themselves and to build up a conscious fighting character." The front page of each issue would challenge American women "to look the world in the face with a go-to-hell look in the eyes." She promised to provide practical advice on contraception. Once she had built an audience of supporters, she would publish her newspaper.

For three months, Margaret spent every waking minute working on the paper. Sitting at the dining room table, she wrote and edited, shaping her words to spread her message. Walking the city streets, she spoke at every meeting and gathering where an audience would listen. Everywhere she went, she left behind advertisements for the *Woman Rebel*.

So far, she had not broken the Comstock Laws. But she would! She wondered who would attack her first.

Her list of opponents was long. Anthony Comstock—because he believed her message was indecent. Doctors—because she was not a doctor and she was talking about medical practice. Men—because she declared that each woman must become the "absolute mistress of her own body." Women—because she encouraged them to rebel against both custom and law. The rich—because she accused them of buying contraceptives illegally. Church leaders—because she violated their rules.

In March, she took bundles of the *Woman Rebel* to the post office.

On April 2, she received a notice from the Post Office Department: the *Woman Rebel* was unmailable.

Front page of the Woman Rebel, *1914*

THE WOMAN REBEL

NO GODS   NO MASTERS

THE FIRST UNVEILED FEMALE HEAD RAISED IN AMERICA

An uncompromising, unapologetic, clear cut, revolutionary paper, dealing with sex education, and advocating a militant attitude toward all things which enslave the working woman.

Study, think, reason, learn thoroughly the elements of a science that all women ought to know: the knowledge of means to prevent conception.

Published monthly.   Subscription $1 a Year.

Address: MARGARET H. SANGER

34 Post Avenue   New York City

She rushed to the post office. Half the copies had been sent, apparently before anyone noticed. The rest had been confiscated.

Why? she asked.

The postmaster general answered that the paper was "indecent, lewd, lascivious, and obscene." If she continued to publish such material, she would be subject to criminal prosecution.

In the next issue, Margaret included a special boxed statement:

> THE WOMAN REBEL FEELS PROUD THAT THE POST OFFICE AUTHORITIES DID NOT APPROVE OF HER.

She continued to write controversial material. In one article, she criticized capitalists for opposing birth control. They were ruining the country, she said, by insisting that women supply workers. In another article, "The Prevention of Conception," she asked: "Is there any reason why women should not receive clean, harmless, scientific knowledge on how to prevent conception?" In the July issue, she asked, "Are Preventive Means Injurious?" Her answer was no.

Then she published an article about the dangers of abortion. That one enraged the postmaster general. He labeled the issue "lewd, vile, filthy, and indecent."

He seized all the copies he could get.

Margaret wanted to get arrested. She was not successful. But she did get lots of criticism. A typical newspaper comment was that the *Woman Rebel* is "a mass of dirty slush."

In churches, offices, and homes, Margaret was criticized, scolded, ridiculed, and scorned. On the other hand, although they did not dare to make public statements, many women felt betrayed. Margaret had promised specific information on birth control, and she had not given it.

On top of that, the seizure of the papers had put Margaret in financial trouble. Subscribers who didn't receive their papers wanted their money back.

Finally in August, Margaret was arrested. Four charges were brought against her. The first three involved breaking obscenity laws. The fourth involved using the mail to "incite murder and assassination." This last charge was made because she published an article titled "In Defense of Assassination." The four charges could bring a sentence of 45 years.

Margaret's trial was set for the fall. She wanted to make the most of the next six weeks of freedom. For the September/October issue of the *Woman Rebel*, she wrote about her coming trial. She scolded citizens for not helping in her cause. She mailed the papers at several different times from several different post offices, successfully avoiding seizure.

Now Margaret had nothing to lose. She was under arrest anyway. She might as well write the brochure that women were asking for. She completed work on *Family Limitation*, her first handbook on birth control. "There must be no sentimentality in this important phase of sexual hygiene," she wrote. With clear and simple language and with diagrams, Margaret described douches, condoms, sponges, and diaphragms. She said that effective contraception would make abortion unnecessary.

In one week, 20 printers refused to handle the job for her. One said, "You'll never get this set up in any shop in New York. It's a Sing Sing job." Another said, "I'd like to set it, but I have a family. I'd be in jail the minute it came out." Finally she found a fellow Socialist who agreed to do the job secretly at night.

Some 100,000 copies were printed. Margaret and her friends spent hours wrapping, weighing, and stamping bundles of pamphlets. With each copy, she included a notice: "Three hundred thousand mothers . . . lose their babies every year from poverty and neglect. . . . Are the cries of these women to be stifled? . . . The women of America answer no!" She gave orders to hold the brochures until the moment was right for distributing them.

When the bundles of *Family Limitation* were safely hidden away, Margaret spent all her time on her coming trial. At her friends' insistence, she hired a lawyer. But when the lawyer told her to plead guilty, she refused. She decided to be her own lawyer. When she asked for a postponement of the trial so she could prepare her case, the judge refused.

She knew that she would be found guilty. This is what she had wanted. She had broken the law in order to get publicity. But now the news was full of war in Europe—World War I had broken out a few months earlier. Margaret Higgins Sanger's case would probably end up on the back pages of the newspapers.

Would she be able to continue her campaign from jail? Probably not. Then what would she gain from a 45-year prison sentence? The answer was *nothing*.

Margaret decided to leave the country to avoid a trial. She felt that she was free to leave her family now. Stuart was away at boarding school. Bill had returned to New York, and he could take care of Grant and Peggy. She did not attempt to say good-bye to her children; perhaps she was afraid that the scene would be too emotional. In Holland and England, Margaret could continue to work on her cause by studying the successful birth control projects there. She would return to America when her trial could receive more attention.

In October 1914, Margaret sneaked onto a midnight train headed for Canada. There she contacted friends of her New York supporters. These new friends supplied her with a passport in the name of Bertha Watson, the alias she would use to elude police. Her passport picture showed a thin wide-eyed woman with a stylish black hat.

From Montreal, Margaret sent supporters a cable, asking them to distribute the bundles of *Family Limitation*.

She sailed out of Montreal Harbor on the R.M.S. *Virginian*. During the week of travel to England, Margaret wrote a letter to her four-year-old daughter:

> *Dear Peggy,*
> *How my heart goes out to you . . . [but] work is to be done, dear—work to make your path easier—and those who come after you.*

Chapter Four

Back to America, Back to Court

1914-1916

During this time . . .
- Electric traffic lights came into use.
- The Coast Guard was created by Congress.
- Henry Ford developed the farm tractor.
- The National Park Service was established.
- New Orleans became well known for jazz.

In England, the two Margarets argued with each other. The Thinking Margaret wondered if she should return to America when Stuart wrote about picking flowers: "I would have sent you some, but you are so far away." Bill wrote that Peggy frantically tried to keep Bill from going to work; her mother had left her abruptly, and Peggy was fearful that her father would do the same. A new heavier cast for her leg also distressed her. Bill wrote that Peggy asked if she could "fly to her mother on wings." The Thinking Margaret worried, but she did not return to her family.

The Emotional Margaret delighted in new friends, new resources for research, and freedom from family responsibilities. Involved in a whole new life, she soon wrote to Bill, asking for a divorce. He wrote back, begging her to reconsider.

Margaret spent time with people who were active in the birth control movement in England. She asked questions, read, and studied. She became less interested in how birth control affected the economy. Instead, she focused on how it affected the rights of women. Women who controlled their reproductive systems had more control over their lives. Their responsibilities were no longer defined by men. Also, they were free to appreciate the beauty of sex.

She studied in the British Museum, sometimes remaining there from nine in the morning until seven at night, reading, thinking, and taking notes.

She learned about the history of family limitation. Four thousand-year-old Chinese medical reports showed doctors using abortion to limit births. Another method of limitation throughout the centuries was infanticide, killing an infant at birth. People also used various combinations of devices and substances to prevent conception. Among substances used to block sperm were honey, olive oil, and alligator dung.

She read about leaders who warned of overpopulation. Thomas Malthus, a British economist (1766-1834), had warned that population was doubling every 15 years in some areas. At this rate, he said, the world would soon run out of food and living space. Francis Place (1771-1854), a labor leader, had declared that large families created more workers than were needed. An oversupply of workers led to low wages and poor working conditions.

Margaret understood why these ideas were less important to Americans than to Europeans. Americans didn't worry about living space. The whole West awaited settlers. They didn't worry about running out of food. Modern machinery enabled farmers to produce more food all the time. New railroad lines made the shipping of food easier and cheaper. They believed that the thousands of immigrants who arrived each year would both furnish workers and create demands for goods.

London psychologist Havelock Ellis and Margaret soon became close friends. She studied his book *Psychology of Sex*. He wrote: "Sex lies at the root of life, and we can never learn to reverence life until we know how to understand sex."

Margaret's life was full of new friends, new thoughts, and new ideas of freedom. She described one special man in her diary as "vigorous, full of confidence, and quick to understand." She no longer had room for Bill in her heart. In December, she wrote to him, saying that she wanted to end the 12-year marriage.

In January 1915, she made plans to go to Holland to visit the world's first chain of birth control clinics. Queen Wilhelmina herself approved of the clinics. Dutch women had the lowest rate of deaths from pregnancy in the world. The rate of deaths in the United States was three times that of Holland.

Dutch doctors recommended that women space their pregnancies at least two or three years apart so that they could regain their health and strength.

Friends tried to persuade Margaret to stay in England. The trip across the English Channel could be dangerous. German submarines patrolled the passage, ready to torpedo ships they suspected of carrying supplies to their enemies, the Allies.

Fear of submarines did not stop Margaret. She made the trip and landed, safe and sound, in The Hague, capital of Holland.

She decided to concentrate on studying. The head

of a birth control clinic encouraged Margaret to enroll in a class for midwives. There, she learned how to fit diaphragms, the contraceptive device most often used by Dutch women. She wrote in a pamphlet, "Dutch Methods of Birth Control," that the purchase of a diaphragm "was looked upon as no more unusual than we in America look upon the purchase of a toothbrush."

Back in America, the birth control movement was making small gains. In 1915, Mary Ware Dennett, a writer, created the first American birth control organization, the National Birth Control League. Dennett's goal for the League was to organize peacefully to change the laws against contraception. At the New York Academy of Medicine, Margaret's supporters arranged an informal discussion of contraception. Doctors spoke in favor of family planning at a meeting of a Chicago settlement house, an establishment that dispensed social services. A well-known doctor from New York, Robert Dickinson, said "we as a profession should take hold of this matter [of contraception] and . . . not let it receive harm by being pushed in any undignified or improper manner."

This news was encouraging to Margaret. However, she was not ready to return to America to face trial.

In January 1915, Bill Sanger had been arrested for

openly distributing *Family Limitation*. Despite problems with their personal relationship, Bill believed wholeheartedly in Margaret's cause. At his trial later, in September, the judge offered him a choice of a $150 fine or 30 days in jail. "I would rather be in jail with my self-respect than in your place without it," Bill answered. Some spectators in the courtroom cheered for him as he was led away to his cell.

Bill wrote to Margaret, warning her not to return to America. He said that the courts were ready to sentence her to five years at hard labor.

Once again, Margaret asked herself if a jail sentence would help the movement. Now she had to consider a new problem. The trip across the Atlantic would be dangerous. German submarines and airplanes threatened ocean traffic. Few captains agreed to make the trip. Those who did worked under frightening restrictions, like dimming ship lights for nighttime travel.

But night after night, Margaret dreamed that Peggy was calling, "Mother, Mother, are you coming back?" In these dreams, the numeral 6 occurred over and over again.

Finally, Margaret could no longer resist her need to see her children. She sailed in September 1915, the month of Bill's trial, and arrived in New York in early

October. The reunion was delightful. Stuart, a teenager, loved sports, especially football. Grant was a serious youngster with a reputation as an excellent student. Peggy was a happy, fun-loving little girl.

All too soon, Margaret had to turn her attention to her indictment. She was still under arrest. Her trial would be called at any moment. She needed ideas, support, and money. Cash was her most crucial need. She could barely support her children, much less pay the expenses of a trial.

For help with court expenses, she turned to the National Birth Control League. To Margaret's surprise, President Mary Dennett spoke against helping her. Dennett argued against the need to break laws in order to change them. She declared that Margaret brought with her an "atmosphere of violence." She also rejected Margaret's idea that only doctors should dispense birth control devices. Margaret believed that this policy would protect women from improper procedures and also would help make birth control more acceptable to the public.

Next, Margaret asked for help from doctors at the New York Academy of Medicine. They also refused, saying they needed more time to consider the issue of birth control. The question was larger than birth control; the male-dominated medical profession wanted to retain control over women's rights to plan their families.

Suddenly, Peggy became ill with pneumonia. Margaret stopped all her other activities to nurse her daughter. She stayed with her day and night for weeks. Neither home nursing nor hospital care helped. On November 6, the five-year-old child died. Margaret wrote in her autobiography, "The joy in the fullness of life went out of it then." The family was in agony with grief. Even years afterward, Margaret found tears in her eyes whenever she saw a child about five years old.

Margaret received letters of sympathy from all over the country. Many were from people who knew her only through newspaper articles and her writing. Some sent donations to help her to continue her work.

Friends feared that Margaret was emotionally unable to withstand a court appearance and the prison sentence that would surely follow. They urged her to compromise with officials to avoid the trial. Some lawyers agreed. They advised her to plead guilty and to promise never to break the law again.

"I'm not concerned about going to jail," Margaret answered. "The question is whether I have or have not done something obscene."

Margaret believed that she should face the court

without a lawyer. The goal of every lawyer was to prove that his client was innocent. Margaret wanted to be found guilty so that she could challenge the Comstock Laws.

She planned to appear in court wearing the "uniform" then commonly worn by feminists—a white shirt, black skirt, and tie. But a friend suggested that she wear a softer, more appealing outfit with a lace collar. He persuaded her to have publicity photos taken wearing this outfit posing with her sons. These photos helped to win sympathy for her throughout the country.

On January 18, 1916, Margaret showed up at the Federal Building in New York, where her trial would take place. Reporters shouted questions. Friends and supporters crowded around to encourage her. People swarmed over the streets. Twenty chauffeured limousines brought wealthy spectators. Some observers came because they were curious about the young woman who dared to fight the district attorney without a lawyer. They wanted to see the expression on her face as she faced trial.

Once seated in the court, everybody waited. Nothing happened for a while. Finally, the judge entered. Immediately, the district attorney requested that the trial be postponed. The judge granted the request.

Again, on January 24, Margaret appeared in court.

1916 publicity photo of Grant, Margaret, and Stuart

Again, lawyers for the prosecution were granted a postponement. On February 14, the case was dismissed. All charges against her were dropped. The prosecutor explained: "We are determined not to let Mrs. Sanger become a martyr.... We are also not the least bit interested in having a public debate on sex theories at this time."

Did Margaret lose? Yes! She lost the chance to test the laws against the distribution of birth control information. She lost the chance to fight for free speech.

Did she win? Yes! She won her freedom. She won admiration and sympathy from people all over the country.

This was the perfect time for a publicity campaign to bring in money and support. The only problem was the same old stage fright that she first experienced at Claverack College.

As a student, she had fought this fear by practicing in front of gravestones. Now she did her practicing on the roof of her apartment. The surrounding roof tops were her audience. In practice sessions, she spoke confidently to the rows of roofs. But when people were her audience, she trembled at the beginning of each appearance, and she was exhausted at the end. She tried reading her speeches, instead of speaking from memory. But she quickly discovered that the audience paid less attention when she read to them. After that, she memorized her talks.

Her audiences never saw her fear. They saw a slim, attractive, self-confident woman. They heard a sure and strong voice insisting over and over: "The first right of every child is to be wanted."

Sometimes she used humor in her talks. She suggested that each baby-to-be should interview the prospective parents. The baby would ask questions about their ability to raise a child. "Eight living in two rooms? No, thank you," the baby would say. "Next applicant, please."

Trains became another home for her. She became familiar with the clang of the fire door as the fireman stoked coal at the beginning of each trip, the moan of the train whistle, and the chuff-chuff of wheels on tracks. Margaret traveled to speaking engagements in Pittsburgh, Cleveland, Chicago, St. Paul, Milwaukee, Detroit, Seattle, and Los Angeles. She organized birth control leagues, raised money, and gained the support of influential people.

In St. Louis, she was scheduled to talk at the Victoria Theater. When she arrived, the theater doors were locked. She learned that officials of the Catholic church had alerted the police that her talk would be both immoral and illegal. The police refused to let anyone enter.

Margaret declared that this was a violation of free speech. She gained support from citizens who strongly approved of freedom of speech, no matter what their attitude toward birth control.

As a result of the publicity, the St. Louis City Men's Club invited her to speak. The club had recently invited former President Theodore Roosevelt to speak. Margaret's audience was larger than Roosevelt's had been.

Chapter Five

The Brownsville Clinic Opens and Closes

1916-1917

During this time . . .
- A fender for a Model T Ford cost $2.50.
- A woman was elected to the House of Representatives.
- "Old MacDonald Had a Farm" became a popular song.
- The United States required literacy tests for citizenship.
- An automobile wrecking crane was devised.

More controversy flared. In Portland, Oregon, men were arrested for selling copies of *Family Limitation*. Margaret and other supporters held a rally to protest the arrests. At the rally, they sold copies of the pamphlet.

Then Margaret was arrested. About 100 supporters

followed her to jail. They begged to be arrested too. Prison officials had to bolt the doors to keep out the crowds.

The next morning, the prisoners were found guilty. Their fines were waived, and they were set free. Once again, Margaret lost the chance to challenge the obscenity law. However, she won a lot of sympathy and publicity.

Margaret continued to ask Bill for a divorce. "There is nothing I have to give you in love, there is nothing to be repaired, there is no way we can go on together," she wrote him. Bill refused to grant the divorce. Margaret's diary shows many romantic attachments, but as she told a female friend, "The kind of man [we] have in mind has not been born."

After three months of touring, Margaret returned to New York. The Emotional Margaret wanted to open a free birth control clinic right away. The Thinking Margaret asked many questions. How would she get enough money? Would women dare to come to the clinic? Would opponents stage demonstrations to keep women away? Would police arrest her as soon as she opened the clinic doors?

She decided to open an office first and to try to work with the state law, not against it. Section 1145 gave doctors the right to prescribe birth control devices and offer information for the "cure and prevention of disease." Physicians used Section 1145 to prescribe condoms for men who sought sex outside of marriage and did not want to contract venereal disease. Margaret planned to hire a physician who would prescribe devices for women for the "cure and prevention of disease" that might accompany a pregnancy.

Margaret set up an office on lower Fifth Avenue. Frederick Blossom, a social worker, agreed to help her with the project. He also paid for some of the office furniture.

The office was immediately swamped with mail. Margaret received 1,000 letters from St. Louis alone. With the help of volunteers, Blossom soon had a system for answering letters. He also knew many rich and influential people, and he persuaded some of them to contribute.

Together, Margaret and Blossom began work on a magazine, *Birth Control Review*, dedicated to discussion of the facts about contraception. Blossom also organized and became president of the New York Birth Control League.

Money and support for a birth control clinic came in. But no doctor wanted to risk his or her career by working at the clinic in possible violation of Section 1145. They all knew the story of Dr. Mary Halton, who had been reprimanded for the "crime" of fitting a diaphragm at a public clinic.

Without a doctor, Margaret had to change her plans. When the birth control clinic would open, she and her sister Ethel Byrne, a nurse, would explain the use of a diaphragm and guess at the correct size for each patient. Then they would give the patient the name and address of a drug store where she could buy the device.

Margaret had a list of druggists to recommend. Most were already selling "womb supporters" and "feminine hygiene" products. The sales were legal even though the druggists probably knew that the devices were used for contraception.

The sisters expected to be raided by the police, but that would not deter them from serving clients. A raid and arrest would give them the chance to fight in court for a doctor's right to prescribe contraceptives for women.

In the worst slums of Brooklyn, Margaret found a storefront that would become the Brownsville Clinic. With a $50 donation from a supporter in Los Angeles, she paid the first month's rent. She brought in a few chairs, a desk, a coal stove, a blackboard, and an examining table. She printed 5,000 pamphlets in English, Yiddish, and Italian, advertising the opening of the clinic.

MOTHERS!

Can you afford to have a large family?
Do you want any more children?
If not, why do you have them?

DO NOT KILL, DO NOT TAKE LIFE, BUT PREVENT

Safe, Harmless Information can be obtained of trained Nurses at

46 AMBOY STREET
NEAR PITKIN AVE. — BROOKLYN.

Tell Your Friends and Neighbors. All Mothers Welcome
A registration fee of 10 cents entitles any mother to this information.

מוטערס!

זייט איהר פערמעגליך צו האבען א גרויסע פאמיליע?
ווילט איהר האבען נאך קינדער?
אויב ניט, ווארום האט איהר זיי?

מערדערט ניט, נעהמט ניט קיין לעבען, נור פערהיט זיך.

זיכערע, אונשעדליכע אויסקינפטע קענט איהר בעקומען פון ערפארענע נוירסעס אין

46 אמבאי סטריט ניער פיטקין עוועניו ברוקלין

מאכט דאס בעקאנט צו אייערע פריינד און שכנות. יעדער מוטער איז ווילקאמען

פיר 10 סענט איינשרייב־געלד זיינט איהר בערעכטיגט צו דיעזע אינפארטיישאן.

MADRI!

Potete permettervi il lusso d'avere altri bambini?
Ne volete ancora?
Se non ne volete piu', perche' continuate a metterli al mondo?

NON UCCIDETE MA PREVENITE!

Informazioni sicure ed innocue saranno fornite da infermiere autorizzate a

46 AMBOY STREET Near Pitkin Ave. Brooklyn

a cominciare dal 12 Ottobre. Avvertite le vostre amiche e vicine.
Tutte le madri sono ben accette. La tassa d'iscrizione di 10 cents da diritto a qualunque madre di ricevere consigli ed informazioni gratis.

Margaret H. Sanger

The Brownsville Clinic flier that was distributed in 1916

In September, a *New York Times* reporter wrote that Margaret Sanger was opening the clinic "despite the fact that the New York law forbids the dissemination of knowledge on the subject."

Margaret and Fania Mindell, a supporter from Chicago, spent hours advertising the opening of the clinic. With Fania, who spoke three languages, acting as interpreter where necessary, they introduced themselves to hundreds of women, and they passed out handbills. They left handbills in letter boxes and under tenement doors.

Early on the morning of October 16, 1916, long lines of women waited for the eight o'clock opening of the Brownsville Clinic. Some held the hands of a couple of toddlers; some pushed wicker baby carriages. Some women came with friends; some came alone. Some came with their husbands' permission; others came secretly. All came seeking an answer to the question: How could they accept responsibility for the sizes of their families?

Over and over, Margaret and Ethel used charts to explain how to insert a diaphragm. When Fania had an extra minute, she read Margaret's "What Every Girl Should Know" articles, bound in pamphlet form, to women in the waiting room.

Fania made notes about each of the more than 100

patients who came to the clinic that first day. One woman told of living in a two-room apartment with only one window. Another said she had only two beds for the seven members of her family. Another spoke of a diet of black bread and black coffee. To Margaret, the most heartbreaking cases were of mothers who were already pregnant and feared that they could not care for another child at that time. Margaret could do nothing for them.

Neighbors around the clinic helped, each in his or her own way. A baker frequently sent doughnuts for the staff. Every day the mailman left with a wave and "I hope I find you here tomorrow." News of the services of the clinic traveled rapidly. Women came from as far away as Massachusetts, Pennsylvania, and New Jersey. For nine days, the three women served long lines of patients. Each day they had to close before all the waiting women were accommodated.

On the tenth day, Mrs. Whitehurst, a "patient" (really an undercover policewoman) from the day before, returned with three plainclothesmen. They seized furniture, supplies, and medical records. They insisted that the frightened patients give their names and addresses. They arrested Margaret and Fania, who were on duty at that time.

The *Brooklyn Daily Eagle* reported that Margaret

lost her temper. The report in the paper showed the Emotional Margaret as she shrieked at Mrs. Whitehurst.

"You dirty thing. You are not a woman. You are a dog."

The policewoman answered, "Tell that to the judge in the morning."

"No, I'll tell it to you now. You dog, and you have two ears to hear me, too," answered Margaret.

Hustled out of the clinic by a police officer, Margaret and Fania were half dragged and half carried to the patrol wagon. Many supporters followed them to the police station.

Margaret was charged with breaking Section 1142 of the Penal Code, which made it a misdemeanor to give out contraception information. Then she was put in a cell at the Raymond Street Jail, where the smell was so foul that she could hardly breathe. The mattress and blankets were filthy. Roaches, bedbugs, and a rat crawled over her at night.

In the morning, well-dressed ladies peered through the cell bars at the prisoners. They introduced themselves as members of a prison reform society. They asked if they could do anything for the inmates.

"Clean up this filthy place," answered Margaret.

The ladies cut their visit short.

At a press conference later that morning, Margaret

told reporters to give taxpayers a message. Their money was being wasted on a disgraceful jail, she said.

She arranged payment of $500 bail, and was freed to await trial. A few weeks later, she started seeing patients again at the clinic.

When the clients came, so did the police. They arrested her again, this time for maintaining a "public nuisance." They forced the landlord to evict her.

The district attorney filed new charges, this time against all three women. He charged both Margaret and Ethel with violating Section 1142. He also charged Margaret with operating a public nuisance. He charged Fania with selling indecent literature, "What Every Girl Should Know."

Margaret seized the opportunity to make a test case of the charges. She wanted to force an answer to the question: May the state interfere with a person's right to life and liberty?

This time she decided to have a lawyer defend her. Attorney Jonah J. Goldstein offered to take the case. Goldstein was well known for his defense of needy and underprivileged defendants. He was an extremely conscientious lawyer, determined to present a perfect case each time he appeared in court.

Margaret received help from the National Birth Control League this time. A group of women, including

Mary Dennett, called themselves the Committee of 100, and they promised to support Margaret. The committee declared that ". . . it is no more indecent to discuss sexual anatomy, physiology and hygiene in a scientific spirit than it is to discuss the functions of the stomach, the heart and the liver."

On November 20, the three women pleaded not guilty. A trial date was set for January, and a panel of three judges was appointed.

On January 8, about 100 women came to court to show support for Ethel, who was being tried that day. Some of these women were part of the Socialist movement that Margaret and Bill had supported earlier. Some were new supporters of the clinic. Many were weighed down with infants, diapers, pacifiers, and food. A *New York Times* reporter wrote about Rose Halpern, who was typical of these women. Mrs. Halpern was "a poorly clad woman with six children ranging in age from sixteen months to ten years." Mrs. Halpern told the reporter that she had come "as a 'demonstration' of the need of information on birth control among the poor." She added that her husband was a garment worker and made only $17 a week.

Ethel admitted in court that she had instructed women about contraception, an act forbidden by Section 1142. Attorney Goldstein argued that this law was

Margaret is greeted by supporters outside the courthouse in Brooklyn where Ethel was about to be tried

unconstitutional because it violated a woman's right to "free exercise of conscience and pursuit of happiness."

The justices refused to hear arguments about constitutionality until Margaret's trial.

On January 22, Ethel was sentenced to 30 days in a workhouse on Blackwell's Island (now Roosevelt Island), a narrow strip of land in the East River. Her term would begin the following day. The judge told her, "The manner in which you violated the law was both deliberate and persistent."

Like her sister, Ethel was quick to seize an opportunity for publicity and drama. "I intend to go on a hunger strike," she announced. She would die for the cause if necessary. She had written her will and arranged for her children to be taken care of. The night before she was imprisoned, she enjoyed a farewell dinner of turkey and ice cream.

Corrections Commissioner Burdette Lewis scoffed at Ethel's statements. He was used to threats of hunger strikes, he said. He would order no food for Ethel. When she wanted to eat, she could ask for it.

She refused to submit to a required physical exam.

"Oh, well, you are clean enough," the prison authorities declared.

Ethel did wear the prison dress of blue-and-white striped gingham.

A *New York Times* reporter who interviewed her in prison wrote:

> *She made an unusually pleasing appearance even in the ugly uniform of the workhouse. She has soft brown hair with a suggestion of curl that gives it a slightly fluffy appearance.*

In the workhouse, Ethel refused to eat. She also refused to drink anything because she feared that any liquid might contain dissolved food. A prison worker came around to the cells regularly, calling

out, "Water!" Ethel never accepted any.

Margaret wrote dramatic press releases about Ethel. She invited reporters to ask questions. News of the hunger strike fascinated readers. Many citizens were more interested in the strike than in the war that was raging in Europe.

Supporters worried about Ethel's health. They feared that officials would allow her to die. Speaking to reporters, Ethel answered with a reference to abortions: "With the Health Department reporting 3,000 deaths a year in the State from illegal operations, one more death won't make much difference, anyway."

This answer worried supporters. On January 25, when Ethel had not eaten for three days, the Committee of 100 spoke to New York Governor Charles S. Whitman. They asked him to help Ethel. He did not answer immediately.

On January 26, prison officials refused to let Margaret visit her sister. Margaret called reporters. "Officialism is running riot," she told them, "when one sister is not permitted to see another who is in a dying condition."

As Margaret expected, this publicity enraged prison officials. On January 27, a doctor and two nurses wrapped Ethel in a blanket so tightly that she could not move. Then they pushed a rubber tube into her

Margaret (left) and Ethel inside the courtroom during the Brownsville Clinic trials

mouth. They put a small funnel on the end of the tube. They poured a mixture of a pint of warm milk, two eggs, and a little brandy into the funnel. They reported that Ethel did not resist the feeding.

Commissioner Lewis received many calls complaining about the forced feeding. To each caller, he answered, "Mrs. Byrne is being fed because the law requires it."

Fania's trial began on January 29. A panel of three justices would preside. There would be no jury. The prosecution had subpoenaed 30 patients from the Brownsville Clinic. They arrived, as ordered, early in the morning. Some carried infants in their arms; others held the hands of toddlers. The mothers waited, caring for the youngsters as well as they could. The children squirmed, played, cried, and fussed. Finally, in the afternoon, the trial began. A few moments later, the case was adjourned until all justices involved could read "What Every Girl Should Know."

Then Margaret's trial began. She sat holding a bouquet of American Beauty roses that someone had handed her as she entered the building. A *New York Tribune* reporter described her as "a demure, rather shy looking woman." He also noted that many smartly dressed society women came to the courthouse to show their support for her.

The first witness was Mrs. Whitehurst, the undercover agent. She reported that Margaret had told her, "I am going to break the law because it is unconstitutional."

The prosecutor then called several mothers, who managed to free themselves of babies, pacifiers, and diapers long enough to take the stand. The prosecutor asked each woman why she had gone to Mrs. Sanger. Each one answered, "To stop the babies." The witnesses smiled at Margaret, obviously pleased with their chance to participate.

Margaret sat quietly. She realized that each answer "to stop the babies" brought her closer to conviction. Finally the court was adjourned for the day.

A *New York Times* reporter quoted a social worker: "Here these poor women [clients] have been ordered to come here and told that if they did not come they would be fined $250 and imprisoned for 30 days.... Both the mothers and the infants have waited all day with nothing to eat."

Newspaper reporters eagerly picked up news about this and other cases involving birth control. Around this time, more than 20 other birth control activists were arrested.

That evening, 3,000 women gathered in Carnegie Hall to start a movement to repeal Section 1142. The group included women of all ages and social classes. Ushers sold copies of the *Birth Control Review* at 15 cents each.

Margaret spoke, describing Blackwell's Island, where Ethel was imprisoned, as a place where "women are tortured for 'obscenity.'" She asked why she should be punished for speaking about family size. Former President Theodore Roosevelt "goes all about the country telling people to have large families, and he is neither arrested nor molested." Why should Margaret Sanger be arrested for suggesting that people might want small families? She criticized doctors who "practice birth control among the women who can pay for it and the poor women can go hang."

At the next session, attorney Goldstein asked the former clinic patients about their families. They told pitiful stories about poverty, infant deaths, and poor health. They were asked how much money their husbands made. A typical answer was: "Ten dollars a week—when he can find work." Many witnesses praised Margaret and the clinic services for helping them to become more responsible and successful wives and mothers.

Finally, one of the judges slammed the gavel. "I can't stand this any longer," he said. He adjourned the court.

On January 31, Margaret and the Committee of 100 visited Governor Whitman. They asked him to create a commission to review Section 1142. He agreed to do so. They also asked him to reduce Ethel's sentence.

"I could grant Mrs. Byrne a pardon only on condition that she would refrain from violating it [the law] upon her release," he answered. He warned that there could be no appeal of her conviction if Ethel were granted a pardon.

The Emotional Margaret was ready to wait for the appeal. "If the State is willing to take a thousand lives to keep a vicious law on the statute books, I am sure my sister is willing that it should take one more," she told reporters.

But the next day, the Thinking Margaret overruled the Emotional Margaret. She asked Governor Whitman to release Ethel right away. "She is in no condition to make any promise," she told him. "But on her behalf, I can promise that she will not again violate the law if she is released."

The governor issued the pardon. On the evening of February 1, Ethel was taken to Margaret's home by private ambulance. Doctors said that they would not know for two weeks if she would recover.

Chapter Six

A Major Victory

1917-1919

During this time...
- ❖An American astronomer measured the Milky Way.
- ❖School attendance became compulsory throughout the U.S.
- ❖Babe Ruth hit a 587-foot home run for the Red Sox.
- ❖Daylight saving time was introduced.
- ❖A woman was elected judge of a juvenile court.

On February 4, Fania was fined $50. The Committee of 100 paid that fine.

At another court session, the district attorney read aloud from *Family Limitation*. He cited the sections where Margaret had written instructions for use of the diaphragm. Margaret was found guilty of violation of

Section 1142. The panel of three judges gave her a choice. They would release her if she would pay a fine and agree not to violate the law again. Or she could accept a sentence of 30 days in the workhouse.

Margaret chose the prison term. Women in the courtroom applauded when she said, "I cannot respect the law as it exists today."

Attorney Goldstein then spoke to Margaret privately and urged her to change her mind. He argued that she should plead guilty and accept a suspended sentence. He warned her that she would get little or no publicity from a jail sentence at this time. News about America's possible entry into World War I dominated the newspapers. News about Margaret Sanger and birth control would be assigned to the back pages.

The judge gave her another chance. "What is your answer, Mrs. Sanger? Is it yes or no?"

In a quiet voice, Margaret answered, "I cannot promise to obey a law I do not respect."

The judge pounded his gavel.

"The judgment of the Court is that you be confined to the Workhouse for a period of thirty days."

Someone in the audience cried "Shame!"

Margaret was taken to a small room to be fingerprinted. She refused to hold out her hands as ordered. She said that fingerprinting was for criminals, for thieves and prostitutes. She was a political prisoner, not a criminal. The officer in charge of fingerprinting conferred with the judge. They decided not to fight her on this point.

Inside the jail, she refused a physical examination. Like the fingerprint clerk, the attendant decided not to fight her.

Joseph McCann, the warden, asked if she wanted lunch. She accepted, assuring him that she would not fast "unless your food is too bad."

In her diary, Margaret wrote of being bored in jail: "afternoon drags slowly and supper—bread and molasses and tea—seemed tasteless"; "dinner of stew and bread"; "afternoon four letters."

Margaret talked to other inmates about understanding their own bodies and about the importance of birth control. The prison matron complained that the inmates knew "bad enough already," but she did not stop Margaret.

Frederick Blossom took over many of Margaret's duties. He continued to publish the *Birth Control Review*, and he included many controversial articles. One article favored restricting immigrants according to their race. The writer spoke against the "melting pot" theory, which encouraged the mixture of races, religions, and customs in America.

Another article focused on a study, "The Cost to the State of the Socially Unfit." The writer declared that only couples who were judged to be intellectually and physically acceptable should be allowed to have children. This eugenicist showed no regard for the value of every human being.

Margaret knew about these articles, and she did not object. She herself had written that "feeble-minded" and "unfit" couples should not have children.

An article in the February issue stated that:

> [excessive pregnancy was] a disease which sends mothers to an early grave, condemns wives to ill health and invalidism, causes children to be born feeble in mind and body, and crushes strong men under the weight of a burden they never asked to carry.

Newsstand owners refused to sell the controversial magazine, just as they had refused to sell the *Woman Rebel*. Blossom sold some subscriptions, and he hired street-sellers to peddle the rest of the copies.

Newsboys stood on busy street corners—opposite Grand Central Terminal, at Times Square, and near Macy's—waving copies of the *Birth Control Review*. Ladies shook their umbrellas, young boys shouted, and sometimes policemen arrested the sellers.

On March 6, the day of Margaret's release from prison, a crowd gathered outside the workhouse early in the morning. They lined a path with flowers.

Then they waited. And waited. And waited. They stood in the cold, and they worried about what might be happening to Margaret. They found out later that Warden McCann had demanded that she be fingerprinted before being released. Margaret refused. The guards had tried to force her fingers onto the ink pad. The struggle lasted over an hour. "I was bruised and exhausted," Margaret told reporters. But she was not fingerprinted.

Finally she walked through the big steel-barred doorway to meet a cheering crowd. Jonah Goldstein and Ethel were among the throng of well-wishers who led her to a hired limousine. Margaret and her friends then celebrated with an elegant breakfast at a nearby restaurant. She called it a wonderful "coming out party." The guests cheered when Margaret told them that attorney Goldstein had filed an appeal to her sentence even though she had already served it.

That afternoon, she attended a luncheon in her honor. That evening she went to see the famous Isadora Duncan in a dance recital. Reporters questioned her as she left the theater. "Already I feel ready to begin work again," she said.

The work she plunged into was movie-making. She and Blossom shot a film titled *Birth Control*, which showed scenes from the opening of the Brownsville Clinic and the problems that followed. Margaret played herself, a nurse caring for a woman who was seriously ill because of repeated abortions.

Again, Margaret asked Bill Sanger for a divorce. Again, he refused. Margaret was busy, too busy to pay much attention to Stuart and Grant. Stuart once walked 20 miles to a train station where he and his mother were to meet. Margaret wasn't on the train; she had no explanation for her absence. Once Grant wrote, "I know you are very busy or you would come to see me." Another time, he wrote, "Now you put down in your engagement book, Nov. 28, Go down to see Grant!"

On April 6, 1917, President Woodrow Wilson announced that the United States would join the Allies in the fight against the Central Powers. American soldiers would soon travel across the Atlantic to take part in World War I.

Margaret immediately fired off an editorial for the *Birth Control Review*. She was a pacifist, a person who believes that no war is acceptable. "I was convinced the primary cause of this war lay in the terrific pressure of population in Germany," she wrote in her autobiography. "She could hold no more [people], and had to burst her bounds."

In the editorial, Margaret accused political leaders of regulating population growth by slaughtering "surplus" people. She demanded that they limit population with birth control instead of with war.

Blossom was enraged. He threatened to resign from the staff if Margaret insisted on what he called a "pro-German" attitude. This was not their first argument, by any means, but it was their fiercest.

When Margaret came into the office one morning, the room was stripped bare. Blossom had taken all the furniture, files, records, and money.

Margaret admitted that he had a right to the furniture, some of which he had paid for. She demanded that he return the records and money immediately. He answered that he needed time to figure out what was rightfully his.

But Margaret needed both funds and records to continue publishing the *Birth Control Review*. She could not wait while Blossom did his figuring, so she hired a lawyer to fight for her. Then Blossom's friends promised that he would cooperate if Margaret would drop the suit. She did so.

Time passed. Blossom did not return the money or the records. Finally Margaret gave up trying to get them back.

The movie *Birth Control* was ready for distribution in July. Before it was released, a judge banned it. In his ruling, the judge said that "the film would have a tendency to arouse class hatred, as it tends to show that the rich have small families and favor the poor having large families." This judgment seemed senseless to many people.

For six months, Margaret did not have enough resources to publish the *Birth Control Review*. Then her sisters lent her the money to start it up again.

The war dominated the news. Americans showed their support for the troops abroad with patriotic speeches and songs. Members of Congress declared that citizens who did not support the war were traitors. Thus, Margaret and other pacifists became traitors.

Support for the birth control movement and other social concerns suffered. Individuals, families, church groups, and social organizations focused on the war.

Some citizens saw birth control as a threat to American strength. In joining the war, America made a commitment to participate in world affairs. This commitment might require a large military and civilian population. Ex-President Theodore Roosevelt, who strongly supported America's participation in the war, urged mothers to have more children: "The race cannot go ahead . . . unless the average man and woman who

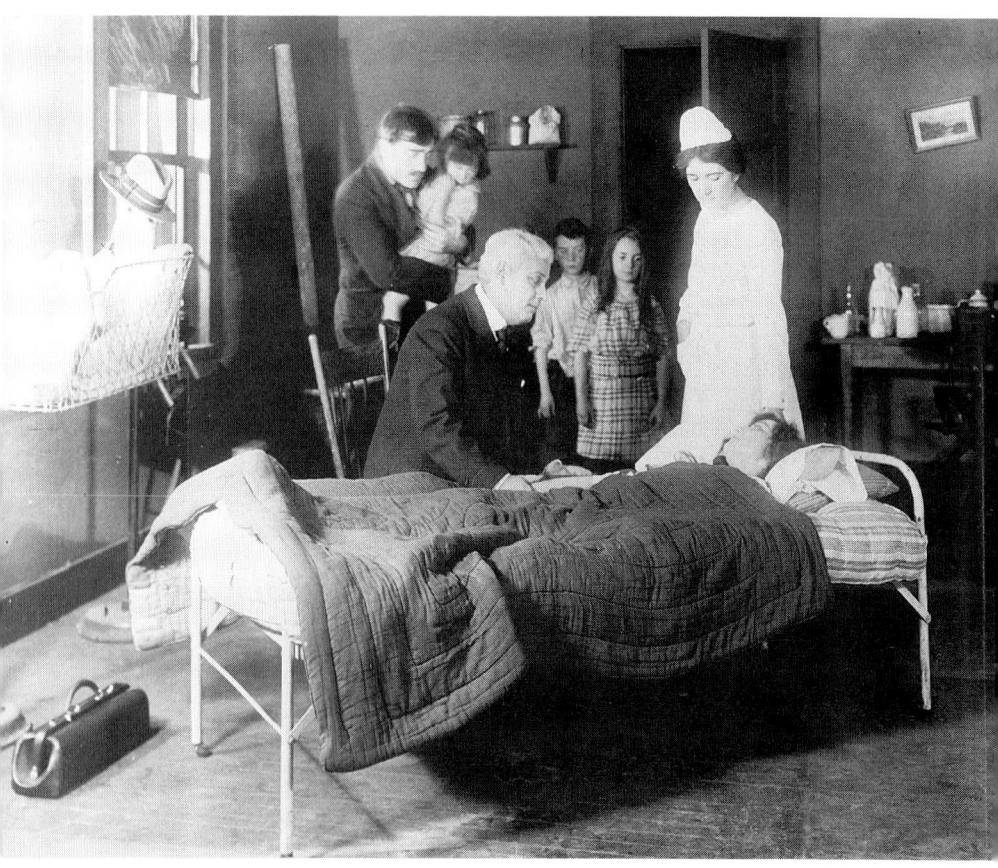

A dramatic scene from Birth Control. *The movie was banned before it could be released.*

are married and who are capable of having children have a family of four children."

Margaret learned that "What Every Girl Should Know" was still in print. In fact, the pamphlet was being used by the United States military, although they had not asked her permission. Military instructors used it to teach soldiers about venereal disease. She did not pursue the matter then. However, she believed that this use by the military effectively removed the label of obscene from the material. She hoped that Fania's conviction would be reversed.

Attorney Goldstein was sometimes Margaret's escort. She called him "Dear, generous one . . . fascinating at times . . ." He also continued as her lawyer, working on the appeal of her conviction.

The answer to that appeal came on January 18, 1918. Margaret lost. The appeals court agreed with the first ruling that Margaret had broken the law by giving out information on contraceptives.

However, a judge of the appeals court offered a new interpretation of Section 1145, the regulation that allowed doctors to prescribe contraceptives "for the cure and prevention of disease." He quoted a Webster's dictionary definition of disease: "any change in the state of the body which causes or threatens pain and sickness."

The judge declared that pregnancy sometimes causes pain and sickness. Therefore, a doctor could legally prescribe contraceptives for prevention of pregnancy. With this new interpretation, the birth control movement won a major victory.

Chapter Seven

A Question of Freedom of Speech

1918-1921

During this time . . .
- ❖ The first Miss America contest was held.
- ❖ The Red Sox sold Babe Ruth to the Yankees for $125,000.
- ❖ Prohibition, the 18th Amendment, making the sale of liquor illegal, went into effect.
- ❖ The 19th Amendment, giving women the right to vote, was passed.
- ❖ A Cadillac cost $2,900.

On November 11, 1918, the Central Powers surrendered to the Allies. Americans, like many people around the world, believed that there would never be another war. Leaders planned a peace conference in Versailles, France, to talk about maintaining a permanent peace.

Margaret in a pensive mood

The world war against aggression was over, but Margaret's war was not. She continued to write letters, give speeches, and travel, always seeking to create and maintain support for her cause. Then her doctor declared that she needed extensive rest, and that she needed it immediately.

She decided to spend three months in Coronado, California. Sixteen-year-old Stuart could not go. He was in prep school, preparing for entrance to Yale. Ten-year-old Grant was delighted with the idea of being away from his boarding school. He missed his mother whenever she was away. Besides, he was tired of being taunted by his friends who called his mother a jailbird.

In California, Margaret worked on a book, *Woman and the New Race*. In it, she said that famine, war, and poverty were caused by overpopulation. She advised laborers to strike against the Comstock Laws, not against their employers. She said that repeal of the Comstock Laws would lower the birth rate, reducing the number of workers to compete for jobs. She suggested that mothers could end war forever by refusing to give birth to "surplus" people.

She declared that responsible birth control would signal the beginning of a superior race. Just as slave mothers brought up slave children, so intelligent and healthy mothers would bring up intelligent and healthy children.

The book was published in 1920. More than 200,000 copies were sold.

That same year, Margaret traveled to Europe. First, she renewed friendships in England. Her special friend was H. G. Wells, a famous English author. Wells said, "When the history of our civilization is written, it will be a biological history, and Margaret Sanger will be its heroine."

As far as Margaret was concerned, her marriage to Bill was over even though he would not consent to a divorce. Bill was not a part of her life emotionally, intellectually, or financially. She had many escorts in England. The Emotional Margaret was attracted to these escorts. The Thinking Margaret believed that she needed her freedom more than she needed the companionship that marriage offered.

She traveled widely in England and Scotland. Everywhere she saw women who were exhausted, sick, emotionally unstable, unable to control their lives and families. She sympathized with them because they lacked inexpensive and easy contraception.

Margaret then traveled to Germany. She wanted to do research on the theory that countries with large populations are forced into war. She believed that the

Germans were an example of this. Around the beginning of the 20th century, there were about 40 million Germans. Less than 20 years later, the population had jumped to 70 million, and German soldiers invaded neighboring lands and started World War I.

German doctors told Margaret that there was no birth control available to women. German women must now produce children to take the places of soldiers and other citizens lost in the war.

Margaret then traveled to France, where she heard much the same story as in Germany. War losses had been great. French women must produce children to make up for them. The government banned contraceptives. Couples who produced many children were sometimes given bonuses by the government.

She worked conscientiously on research and study, but Margaret felt ill throughout the European trip. When she returned to London, she made an appointment with a doctor. He found that she had a touch of tuberculosis beneath her tonsils. She underwent surgery to take care of the problem.

She arrived in New York in November. She planned a Thanksgiving dinner for Bill, Ethel, Grant, and Stuart. The boys were awkward with both Bill and Margaret because they saw so little of their parents. Bill was awkward for another reason, as he explained in a letter to Margaret after the dinner:

> *Please don't invite me again. I sat across the table from you and still loved you so much I couldn't bear it.*

In early 1921, Margaret spoke about opening another birth control clinic, this one on the East Side of Manhattan. J. Noah Slee, a partially retired executive in the Three-in-One Oil Company, was interested, both in the clinic and in the auburn-haired activist who was planning it. He became Margaret's frequent companion.

Margaret and Slee had little in common. She was 42 years old; he was 60. She was an atheist; he was a former superintendent for St. George's Sunday School. She was a Socialist; he was a Republican. She was always scrabbling for money to pay her bills; he was a millionaire.

Slee sent flowers and notes to her home every day. She liked to dance, so he took dancing lessons at Arthur Murray's. He bought an addressograph and installed an up-to-date filing system for her office. He set up a system for answering the heavy volume of mail.

When Margaret received her divorce from Bill (on grounds of desertion), Slee asked her to marry him. She refused. The Emotional Margaret was intrigued by the courtship. The Thinking Margaret told a friend that she wasn't interested in marriage. She was "no fit person for love or home or children or friends or anything which needs attention or consideration."

With Noah on the edges of her mind, Margaret prepared for the First American Birth Control Conference in November 1921. She invited prominent social scientists, physicians, reformers, and everyone who had supported her in the past. In her advertisements and announcements, she warned that overpopulation causes unemployment, poverty, crime, and war. She challenged participants to offer realistic solutions to overpopulation.

As one part of the conference, Margaret rented a room in the Plaza Hotel to show birth control methods to doctors and nurses. One thousand participants came to that session. The medical people, most of whom had earlier argued against contraception, listened with close attention.

To conclude the conference, she hired Town Hall on West 43rd Street for a mass public meeting. She titled her lecture "Birth Control! Is It Moral?" She invited religious leaders of all denominations.

She tried not to think about her fear of public speaking. In her autobiography, she later admitted: "My nervousness ahead of lectures continued to be akin to illness. All through the years it has been like a nightmare even to think of a pending speech."

The Town Hall lecture was to begin at 8:30 P.M. As Margaret's taxi drew close to the hall that night, she held her breath with excitement. The streets were so jammed with cars that the taxi could not move.

Margaret was ecstatic. This would be an overflow meeting!

She and her friends left the taxi and made their way through shouting crowds to the hall. There a policeman told her that the meeting had been canceled. Margaret called police headquarters. The officer who answered said he knew nothing about the meeting.

One hundred policemen surrounded the locked doors of the hall. Suddenly, the police discovered that some people were already inside. They opened the doors to let them out. When the doors opened, a crowd rushed in. Margaret was in that crowd.

She jumped to the stage.

"I'm Margaret Sanger," she shouted. "Get in out of the aisles."

The crowd clapped as they moved into their seats.

A supporter gave her a bouquet of American Beauty roses. "Here's Mrs. Sanger," he yelled.

Suddenly a woman rushed to the stage. She read

a message from Monsignor Dineen, secretary to Archbishop Patrick J. Hayes of New York City's St. Patrick's Cathedral. The message said that the hall must be cleared at once.

The crowd sat stunned.

Margaret jumped to center stage to begin the meeting. Police surrounded her, trying to push her off the stage.

"Why?" she asked. They did not answer.

As fast as police pulled would-be supporters off the stage, new supporters jumped up. Some policemen tried to herd the audience out of the hall.

Police Captain Donohue came to the platform with Monsignor Dineen. "The meeting must be closed," said the monsignor. "An indecent, immoral subject is to be discussed."

Captain Donohue agreed.

The Emotional Margaret made a quick and dramatic decision. She had to be arrested! This was her chance to test freedom of speech.

Ten times she tried to speak. Ten times she was stopped. Finally, Captain Donohue arrested her.

Police escorted Margaret and three women supporters outside. The sidewalks and streets were full of police, supporters and opponents of birth control, and curious onlookers.

Margaret refused to ride in the patrol wagon. Carrying the bouquet of roses, she strode to the station surrounded by policemen. Several hundred men and women marched behind them singing "My Country 'Tis of Thee." She was booked on charges of disorderly conduct, and released.

The investigation that followed found Margaret innocent. A police captain was found guilty of sending in his men without due cause.

Newspaper headlines soundly criticized both the police and the church. The *World* declared: "The issue is bigger than the right to advocate birth control. It is part of the eternal fight for free speech."

Catholic church officials reacted from their pulpits. Archbishop Hayes said, "Children troop down from heaven because God wills it... to prevent life that the Creator is about to bring into being is satanic."

Margaret announced another meeting, at the Park Theater in Columbus Circle. Thousands crowded into the 1,500-seat theater that night. Three thousand people were turned away for lack of room. Some climbed fire escapes to try to sneak in.

Margaret spoke quietly and calmly for just ten minutes. The crowd interrupted her with loud applause 19 times.

"It is not only inevitable, but it is also right that we

learn to control the size of our family, for by this control and adjustment we can raise the standards of the human race," she told the audience.

She spoke in direct opposition to the centuries-old Catholic church teaching that sexual union was acceptable only for the purpose of producing children: "I contend that it is just as sacred and beautiful for two people to express their love when they have no intention of being parents, and that they can go into that relationship with the same beauty and the same holiness with which they go into music or to prayer."

Chapter Eight

A New Clinic, A New Husband

1921-1925

During this time . . .
- Iced treats were named Popsicles.
- The first Macy's Thanksgiving Day parade was held.
- One-third of U.S. households had telephones.
- A postcard cost a penny.
- A baseball game was broadcast on the radio for the first time.

Margaret now received more invitations to speak than she could handle. Before, she had been lucky to receive $50 and expenses for a speech. Now offers came in as high as $1,000.

In 1922, Margaret published *The Pivot of Civilization*. With this book and *Woman and the New Race*,

Margaret earned a respectable amount of money for her writing. In *The Pivot of Civilization*, she wrote, "An overwhelming proportion of classified feebleminded children in the New York schools come from large families. . . ." Again, she recommended that physically or mentally incompetent people should be forced, if necessary, to use birth control. She said that this regulation would lead to fewer "misfits" in society. She agreed with eugenicists that governments should have some control over childbearing. Again, she was raising the idea that some human lives have more value than others.

Margaret was little concerned when the National Birth Control League broke up. She had disagreed with their goals for several years. She was not interested, either, in a new organization, the Voluntary Parenthood League. Like the NBCL, this organization wanted to repeal federal statutes but would not contest them by breaking the law. Margaret had no patience with what she considered less than total involvement.

She received an invitation to participate in a lecture series in Japan. Albert Einstein, Bertrand Russell (a British philosopher), and H. G. Wells were other speakers in this series. She was delighted to accept. She had often warned that Asian countries, with their rapidly expanding populations, were a threat to world peace.

In February 1922, Margaret, Grant, and Noah Slee met in San Francisco, preparing to sail on the *Taiyo Maru*. When Margaret asked for a visa to enter Japan, the consul refused. The emperor had heard of her arrests and considered her an undesirable person. Besides, he believed that she would speak on an improper topic.

Margaret had an idea. She applied for and received a visa for China. The *Taiyo Maru* was going there after it landed in Tokyo, Japan. She planned to persuade officials to let her off in Japan.

In Tokyo, Margaret sent a message to the American consul asking for permission to land. Before she received a reply, Japanese officials questioned her extensively. When they left, reporters took up the questioning. One group of women from the New Woman's Society of Japan also came to see her. They explained why they supported her:

> *When leaders say women need the vote, most women do not listen. When they say women need economic equality, most do not listen. But when they hear of birth control, then like lightning we understand.*

Finally, the U.S. consul sent word that she would be allowed to disembark if she would agree to comply with the conditions set by the Japanese officials. The conditions were that Margaret not describe specific birth control techniques. She might speak only on the social and economic effects of family planning. Margaret agreed.

In Japan, Margaret's public speaking skills were put to the test: She followed the Japanese custom of speaking for about five hours at a time. One of her talks was to the Diet, the Japanese parliament.

Margaret was delighted when Japanese officials made plans for a permanent birth control committee. A publisher planned to bring out a Japanese edition of *Family Limitation*.

Next, she traveled to China, where she saw agonizing poverty. She wrote that the millions of starving Chinese "were the best argument in the world for birth control."

From Asia, Margaret, Slee, and Grant traveled to Egypt, Venice, Paris, and London.

In London, Margaret agreed to marry Slee. However, she insisted on several conditions: She would have a private area for herself in their home; she would keep her own name; Slee would never question her about what she was doing or where she was going. Slee signed the agreement, declaring that Margaret was "the greatest adventure of my life."

The private ceremony was held in London in the fall of 1922. Margaret wore green silk and jade jewels. Noah wore a black suit, a white vest, and a gardenia in his lapel. A justice of the peace performed the ceremony.

Margaret wanted to keep the marriage a secret as long as possible. Neither divorce nor remarriage was acceptable in American society. Margaret was afraid that the news would hurt her cause. Besides, Noah himself was divorced only weeks before the ceremony.

When the couple arrived back in Manhattan, they moved into an apartment on Fifth Avenue near Washington Square. They also planned and built a large home, which they called Willowlake, near the Hudson River in upstate New York. This home was large enough for Margaret to have a separate apartment.

Noah found himself drawn into Margaret's work at the American Birth Control League. He gave thousands of dollars. He used his business background to help with financial records.

Tens of thousands of letters came into the clinic each month. Some typical letters were:

Being married about four years have 3 children and seem as I am pregnant again and so weak can't hardly get around and just think three babies to take care of . . .

> *Our Dr. told my husband to get a divorce as I could not stand having children, but we are happy together with our boys and won't do anything like that . . .*

Clinic workers included a copy of *Family Limitation* with each response. But Margaret knew that learning about a diaphragm was useless for a woman unless she could find a doctor who would prescribe and fit the device and could also obtain the money to pay the doctor's fee.

Margaret believed that she could open a clinic that would take care of these two problems. Once again, she planned to hire a doctor who would prescribe contraceptives for women "for reasons of health" that were related to pregnancy. She planned to seek private funding to pay charges for women who could not afford the service.

Dr. Dorothy Bocker, who worked for the Public Health Service in Georgia, agreed to serve in the clinic. Margaret warned her that she might be arrested. Dr. Bocker accepted the position anyway.

Once again, Margaret sought money and public support.

Again, the labor movement disappointed her. Workers were fighting for higher wages and better working conditions. She could not convince them to fight for women's rights.

Social workers also refused to support the project. Their roles, they said, did not extend to help with family planning.

Many men and women opposed her because they believed that she was violating the holiness of motherhood. A typical opinion is found in one woman's letter to Margaret: "Naturally, we all appreciate the fact that we would be free from having children, but it only . . . gives married women a freedom to wander more into the sin of the world."

Margaret didn't give up. She found two supporters who together contributed $6,000. This was enough for Dr. Bocker's salary for the first year, an examining table, a sterilizer, and other equipment.

She rented an office on Fifth Avenue. The new organization became the Birth Control Clinical Research Bureau. Although Margaret thought of the project as a clinic, not a bureau, she could not use the word *clinic*. New York State law dictated that each clinic had to be associated with a hospital. Margaret knew that no hospital would associate with her.

In January 1923, she opened the doors. By the end of February, 2,700 women had registered for services. Dr. Bocker had fitted 900 women with diaphragms after certifying that each of these fittings was necessary for "health reasons."

Now Margaret faced a new problem. She could not get all the diaphragms she needed. The law on manufacture and supply was vague. Few businessmen dared to make or sell them on the open market. Margaret had to rely on supporters who smuggled them in from Europe. When they had a shipment, they would call the bureau. "Your jewels have arrived" was their code for a supply of diaphragms.

Then she happened to talk to Vito Silecchia, the man who supplied her with coal for her fireplace. Prohibition had banned the sale of liquor in the United States, and Vito made a lot of money smuggling in liquor from Europe. He offered to do the same with diaphragms. Noah joined the arrangement. If Vito would bring back gin for him as well as diaphragms for Margaret, Noah would lend Margaret the money to pay Vito. It was a deal!

At the bureau, Margaret kept careful records of patients. Eventually the Birth Control Clinical Research Bureau became a rich source of information for doctors, social workers, and clergymen. She asked questions about national origin, occupation and income, religion, housing, and number of pregnancies. One interesting discovery was that living conditions sometimes determined the method of contraception. Inserting and caring for diaphragms required privacy; a woman who shared a bathroom with several families did not have this luxury.

Unfortunately, Dr. Bocker did not keep the same careful records as Margaret did. Dr. Robert Dickinson of New York, working on research of his own, declared publicly that Bocker's research was not reliable. Margaret investigated and then fired Dr. Bocker.

She hired Dr. Hannah Stone to take Dr. Bocker's place. Dr. Stone was a warm and sympathetic person, dedicated to helping women. In order to prescribe the diaphragm widely, she compiled a long list of conditions that she believed indicated that pregnancy might be harmful. One condition was that the woman had a baby younger than nine months. A less specific condition was that the woman's present life was too psychologically demanding to allow her to accept more stress.

When she couldn't find an "acceptable" medical reason, Dr. Stone prescribed the device and wrote NHR (No Health Reason) on the record. She was aware that she could be arrested for prescribing contraceptives for a patient labeled NHR.

Dr. Stone and her fellow clinic workers were not alone in their support of birth control. More and more women volunteered to promote the *Birth Control*

Supporters selling copies of the Birth Control Review, *1925*

Review. An international movement was growing. In 1925, move than 1,000 delegates from 18 countries attended the International Birth Control Conference in New York. At that meeting, a leader of the American Medical Association said, "Women have a right to know how they can intelligently—not crudely and

dangerously—control their sexual lives."

At the conference, Dr. Stone discussed the records of the Birth Control Clinical Research Bureau. She cited statistics about many aspects of patients' lives. They showed that 38 percent of the clinic's patients were Protestant, 32 percent were Jewish, and 26 percent were Catholic. Clients came for both economic and health reasons. Her records showed that the diaphragm was 98 percent effective.

The *Medical Journal and Record* reviewed her reports. This review marked the first time that birth control was discussed in a leading professional magazine. The birth control movement was becoming more socially acceptable.

Things were beginning to change. Women began to take on new roles and attitudes. For generations, typical women were heavyset, maternal, completely involved in homemaking. Little girls wanted to grow up like them. Now a new generation of young women wanted to be slender and stylish. Electricity, cleaning aids, packaged foods, ready-to-wear clothes all helped to give homemakers more time outside the home. Women discovered that they had time to work on causes, to hold part-time jobs, and to enjoy some personal freedom. A new style of advertisement showed women shopping, dancing, and riding in open cars.

Margaret continued to travel widely, usually without Noah. He sent adoring letters, telling her of his loneliness. Sometimes she answered in the same tone: "England is nothing without my adorable lover husband." At other times, she seemed to forgot about Noah as she attracted other escorts.

Chapter Nine

A Raid on the Research Bureau

1925-1929

During this time . . .
- ❖ *The Jazz Singer*, the first "talkie" movie, was shown.
- ❖ The Harlem Globetrotters were organized.
- ❖ The last horse-drawn fire engine was retired.
- ❖ Mickey Mouse films appeared.
- ❖ Penicillin, the "wonder drug," was discovered.

Noah helped with more than money. He also smuggled diaphragms through Canada by train in boxes labeled Three-in-One Oil. A customs officer became suspicious about the weight of the cartons. He discovered the diaphragms, and he seized the shipment. Because Noah was such a well-known businessman, he was let off with a promise not to commit this crime again.

Luckily, Margaret had a friend who decided to manufacture diaphragms secretly in the United States.

The Slees' lovely home, Willowlake, attracted many visitors, including children of both their families. Stuart visited from Yale, and Grant from a boarding school. They called their stepfather Pater, and Noah was generous and loving toward them. Noah's two grown sons and a daughter often joined the family there. Together, they rode horses, swam in the lake, and enjoyed the large estate. Soon, Noah's grandchildren also became part of the happy Willowlake vacations.

Margaret's book *Happiness in Marriage* was published in 1926. In it, she said, "Marriage no longer means the slavish subservience of the woman to the will of man." She told couples not to argue because "petty quarrels inevitably lead to more serious ones." She also said that couples should practice birth control so that childbirth would be "not a penalty or a punishment but the road by which she [woman] travels onward toward completely rounded self-development." A *New York Times* review praised the book for its advice.

In her mid-40s, Margaret worked both at home and at the clinic, and she continued to travel to give talks. In Denver, Colorado, a reporter wrote: "Margaret Sanger came into view, younger and lovelier than on her first visit. . . ." In her talks, Margaret was energetic and attractive. She hooked her audience with stories of women who had written to her about their problems. The audience never guessed that she was nervous about speaking.

In 1927, she devoted herself to planning an international conference on population control in Geneva. This Swiss city was the home of the offices of the League of Nations, an organization of countries dedicated to peace. She hoped that speakers at her conference would influence League of Nations policies and programs.

She spent months in Geneva, raising money, rounding up speakers, inviting delegates, and making arrangements for facilities.

Noah had objected to her going off without him. To make up for her absence, she wrote frequent letters:

Dearest Noah–Darling

It's really always lonely to be away from you even one day . . .

You see, Noah dear, all my life I have acted on an inner voice and when that speaks to me, it speaks wisely and never fails me. . . . If only I could help you to believe this. . . .

Some of her letters to Noah spoke of loneliness. A letter to a friend showed something else: "I have had my hand kissed by every nation of Europe and Asia except Italy . . . and [I] have now decided never to live in the USA longer than I can help it."

Three days before the opening of the conference, the chairman, Sir Bernard Mallett, and Margaret went over the final program notes. Mallett crossed out the names of all the women who had worked on the conference. They had no place in a scientific program, he said. "These distinguished scientists would be the laughingstock of all Europe if it were known that a woman had brought them together."

Margaret was enraged. She called a meeting of all the women who had worked on the program. The women reacted as she had—with anger. They wanted to boycott the conference. Margaret hesitated. The Emotional Margaret felt that a boycott would be a fine dramatic show. The Thinking Margaret realized that a boycott would probably doom the conference to failure. Without the women to run it, the organization of the conference would break down. All their planning and work would be wasted. They would lose the opportunity to publicize the importance of population control. With some regret, Margaret persuaded the women to return to work.

The result was a successful conference that established the International Union for the Scientific Investigation of Population.

Margaret stayed in Europe for the following Christmas. She wrote to Grant: "When this letter reaches you it will be 1928. We both wish you a happy & joyous & fruitful New Year. . . . I am keen to learn how you enjoyed your holidays & especially to hear just where you and Stuart went."

When she arrived back in New York, she worked with others on a new book, *Motherhood in Bondage*, a collection of letters sent to the Clinical Research Bureau. The letters showed the despair and desperation of the women who were seeking help.

Besides writing, Margaret served as president of the American Birth Control League. Frequently, though, she began to disagree with its changing policies. The ABCL had a new board of directors, and it was becoming a public service organization, intent on pleasing the public. It disapproved of demonstrations, assertiveness, and conflict.

Margaret also disagreed with the organization's changes in financial procedures. In the past, she had made her plans, and then she had tried to figure out how to fund those plans. The new board of directors worked the other way around. They established a budget first, and then they decided which plans they could afford.

Margaret learned about another change when she ordered renewal slips for *Birth Control Review* subscriptions. She was told that she had to get permission to buy anything costing over $5.00. Always impatient with such office details, Margaret was frustrated and angry.

Margaret resigned as president of the American Birth Control League. She agreed to remain as editor of the *Birth Control Review*.

But there, too, she ran into conflict. Margaret no longer had complete control of the publication. She was one member of a board of five women. In 1929 she resigned from both the *Birth Control Review* and the American Birth Control League.

Both opposition and support for the movement grew louder. In February 1929 a public hearing was held in the Assembly chambers in Albany. More than 1,000 people crowded the hall to hear a debate on proposed legislation that would permit doctors to offer birth control information to married people. After heated arguments, the proposed legislation failed.

A few weeks later, Margaret was invited to speak at a meeting in Boston. Mayor James Michael Curly threatened to take away the license of Ford Hall if

Margaret spoke there. Margaret made a dramatic appearance. But she didn't speak a word. She stood on the stage of the auditorium with her mouth taped. Historian Arthur Schlesinger, Sr., read a short statement that she had written: "I see immense advantages in being gagged. It silences me, but it makes millions of others talk and think about the cause in which I live." Schlesinger called Margaret the "outstanding social warrior of the century." Reporters gleefully snapped photos.

Not all her appearances were so dramatic. One woman supporter described her: "small, quiet, elegant in a stone beige coat trimmed with black Persian lamb. . . . Her voice, calm and quiet, answered questions without fuss. . . ."

Margaret continued to please audiences. Another woman said: "I was intrigued by the delightful, petite, extremely feminine woman with lovely red hair who poured out her heart to the packed audience. . . . It was not delivered as a militant crusade, but with the sincerity, the appeal, of a woman's compassion for all women who were longing to be free from slavery to their biological functions. . . ."

In April 1929, police raided the Clinical Research Bureau. Margaret was at home, caring for Stuart, who was ill at the time.

Margaret gagged on stage in Boston's Ford Hall

When she received the call about the raid, Margaret left Stuart with a maid and rushed to the bureau. She found a police car parked in front, the office blinds down, and a locked door. She demanded that a policeman let her in.

The scene inside was reminiscent of the Brownsville Clinic raid 13 years before. Some police officers were questioning frightened clients. Others were seizing books and supplies. Still others took the records of more than 150 patients.

Two doctors and three nurses (not including Margaret) were accused of breaking Section 1142 of the Penal Code by giving a patient information about contraceptives. That "patient" was an undercover policewoman who had visited the bureau the day before.

Margaret went to the police station with the accused clinic workers. They were freed after paying a $300 bail and agreeing to appear for a hearing the following Friday.

The New York County Medical Society and representatives of the New York Academy of Medicine formally protested against the police action. Although most doctors opposed Margaret's work, in this case they were concerned that the right to keep medical records confidential was being put at risk.

At the hearing, defense attorney Morris Ernst

asked a clinic doctor if contraceptives were often prescribed to prevent disease.

"You say often; I say always," replied the doctor.

Spectators cheered.

A little later, the judge criticized the clinic for carelessness. He said the staff did not take enough care to find out if clients were married.

Attorney Ernst asked, "Do you know of any case in medicine where a doctor sends out detectives to find out about a patient?"

Spectators laughed.

The angry judge cleared the room of spectators.

Attorney Ernst argued that the doctors and nurses had given advice on preventing disease in good faith with the aim of promoting good health. The prosecution argued that the advice was not meant to prevent disease but to prevent pregnancies.

The New York *Herald Tribune* reported: "If the police can seize doctors' files without a specific warrant . . . the possibilities of abuse, including blackmail, are virtually unlimited." The New York Academy of Medicine called the raid a threat to the "freedom of the medical profession."

On May 14, the bureau was cleared of all charges. Margaret made a public statement: "This decision will put the birth control movement ahead many years."

Chapter Ten

Committee on Federal Legislation

1929-1937

During this time . . .
- ❖ Popeye became a popular cartoon character.
- ❖ Hostess Twinkies appeared in grocery stores.
- ❖ Cars used windshield wipers.
- ❖ Knock-knock jokes were popular.
- ❖ Millions of Monopoly sets were sold across the nation.

Perhaps the widely publicized case against the bureau encouraged would-be supporters. Across the country, new clinics appeared—in Detroit, Philadelphia, San Francisco, and Los Angeles. Margaret continued to make appearances all over the country.

While she was traveling, she received romantic

notes from Noah: "Come home soon please. I need you to clasp in my arms always, and love divinely always more and more." Sometimes he shared her excitement; sometimes he was jealous of the time she spent away from him. Once he wrote, "I hate B.C. [birth control] that takes you away."

By the end of 1929, the bureau was serving 20,000 patients annually. Each year, 5,000 new patients sought help. The bureau also served physicians who came to learn how to fit diaphragms. Confidently, Margaret declared that the bureau "would lead woman out of darkness and despair into the light of sane living."

Soon the offices were no longer big enough. Noah bought a five-story town house in Manhattan for $80,000. He and Margaret renovated it—turning the large parlors into examining rooms. They also set up rooms for consultation and treatment as well as a playroom for children. Eighteen hundred patients came to this new office complex each month.

In 1931 Margaret set up headquarters for the National Committee on Federal Legislation for Birth Control (NCFLBC) in Washington, D.C. The committee would fight by lobbying in Congress for laws that would allow doctors to disseminate birth control information and devices to any patient. The time seemed right for a new attack on the law. American attitudes toward sex were changing rapidly. In that year, the President's Committee on Social Trends studied popular magazines. They found that two-thirds of the opinions expressed about birth control were favorable.

New York's Academy of Medicine declared that "the public is entitled to expect counsel and information on the important and intimate matter of contraceptive advice."

In 1930 and 1931 more lenient attitudes on birth control were accepted by the American Unitarian church, the Quaker church, the Universalist church, the Congregational church, the Presbyterian church, and the Central Conference of American Rabbis.

However, Pope Pius XI declared that any form of birth control "violates the law of God and nature, and those who do such a thing are stained by a grave and mortal flaw."

Margaret spent most of her time accumulating endorsements, attempting to persuade legislators to attach pro-birth control riders to welfare bills, organizing state-by-state pressure on legislators, and speaking to raise money and support for the National Committee on Federal Legislation for Birth Control. She wrote to Grant about her busy schedule:

We leave Thurs. March 13 for Denver—I speak

> there and leave for Chicago again the same night. Wild again! Arrive Chicago the 17th and leave for Madison, Wis. at once. Then up to Minneapolis (to speak) for 18th and 19th—then back to Oberlin College and cross again to St. Louis for the 23rd. . . .

Grant answered that he missed her. "As I grow older, I appreciate you more," he wrote.

These were difficult economic times. In the 1930s, one out of every four workers was unemployed. Margaret was quick to point out that birth rates for families on welfare were almost 50 percent higher than those for families with at least one employed worker.

Margaret was able to persuade a few congressmen to introduce bills. But time after time, a bill was sent to a committee where it died, was tabled with no action, or was defeated outright.

With the help of a couple of journalists, Margaret published an autobiography, *My Fight for Birth Control*. She was proud of her accomplishments, and she didn't hesitate to say so. Reviewers liked the book. The New York *Herald Tribune* said that Margaret was "one of perhaps a half-dozen or so whose individual lives swerve or push the course of the world in a direction it might not know at that time except for them."

Politics took over the headlines in 1932. People were interested in the upcoming presidential election between Democrat Franklin Roosevelt and Republican Herbert Hoover. They were also involved in debates about Prohibition, the national ban on liquor.

Eleanor Roosevelt, Franklin's wife, had supported Margaret and her work earlier. In 1932, when Roosevelt was elected president, Margaret expected him to support her. He refused because, he said, the financial problems of the country were his top priority. He did not agree that birth control might help to solve some of those problems.

Margaret answered, "I'm getting sick of this stupid country."

Noah lost much of his money because of the Great Depression. He was devastated personally as well as professionally. Margaret seized the opportunity to become more independent. She took on the challenge of supporting herself with lectures and writing. This financial independence changed her attitude toward the marriage. She felt less obligated to spend time with her husband. Although they exchanged many loving letters, Margaret grew increasingly distant from him.

In the spring of 1933, Margaret called Noah from Washington, asking him to join her in a short vacation in Bermuda. He shouted back over the phone that she "was wasting her life on a cause no one cared about, except a bunch of nuts." He complained that she wanted him only when she needed a favor.

Margaret had no time to fret about a missed vacation. She continued to work, directing many projects. One was to attract public attention with pamphlets using cartoon characters to show the advantages of birth control. Another project was to encourage supporters to write one letter every month to their members of Congress. Margaret also sent many letters. At the top of her stationery was the motto "Every Child a Wanted Child." But it was not easy to change attitudes on Capitol Hill.

One lobbyist, Hazel Moore, told a congressman ". . . if two million men had a toe ache within the last 60 years they would appropriate millions of dollars to care for them . . . but because two million women had died from childbirth and God only knew how many from abortions . . . they didn't have time to put a bill in a box and let us arrange for a hearing."

As the Depression deepened, more couples who did not use contraception turned to illegal abortions. The need for contraception seemed even more immediate.

Margaret devised a new plan of attack. She asked a Japanese physician to send 120 diaphragms to Dr.

Stone. As she expected, U.S. customs officials seized the package. Attorney Ernst, acting for Dr. Stone, filed a suit claiming that the government could not restrict the importation of devices intended for legitimate medical use.

Margaret's case, which came to trial two years later, was not the only one against customs. Also pending were decisions on contraceptive devices seized at other times, a box of contraceptive literature and materials, a report of the International Medical Group, and some books including *Practices of Contraception* and *Rhythm*.

While awaiting trial, Margaret continued to push for legislation, encouraged women to support her, and sought funding for the cause. Not everyone found her easy to work with. One volunteer said, "Margaret, were she not so gentle except when frustrated, was rather like a lion tamer. She kept us each on our boxes until she needed us—then we jumped and jumped fast." Some women who worked for Margaret complained about her. They said that she did not include them in decisions, paid them poorly, and complained often about their inefficiency.

Dr. Stone's case concerning the mailing of diaphragms finally came to trial. Dr. Stone alleged that she used the diaphragms for experimental purposes, to "determine the reliability and usefulness of contracep-

tives to cure and prevent disease." Attorney Ernst argued that she had a right to receive diaphragms since she had a right to prescribe them. The judge agreed. The government appealed.

The Second Circuit Court of Appeals upheld the judge's decision. Margaret celebrated this as the "greatest legal victory in the Birth Control Movement."

For months, the National Committee on Federal Legislation for Birth Control sent out pamphlets and letters, telling doctors about the new ruling. Workers

Margaret (center) at the Tucson, Arizona, birth control clinic, 1936

contacted public health agencies, urging them to offer birth control counseling to their clients. Then Margaret dissolved the NCFLBC; it had met its goal.

With the new ruling in place, Margaret declared that women needed ten times more family planning clinics than were available. She estimated that the country needed 3,000 clinics in all. "We need caravans of education and help for mountain women, farm women, mothers on distant homesteads, mothers in all districts, city and country, who are now neglected."

Margaret at the stove in her Arizona home

Chapter Eleven

A Better World

1937-1966

During this time . . .
- ❖ The ballpoint pen was invented.
- ❖ Walt Disney's *Pinocchio* was released.
- ❖ Teflon was developed.
- ❖ The Barbie doll was introduced.
- ❖ The first McDonald's opened.

In 1937 Margaret was advised by her doctor to slow down—she was 58 years old and had recently undergone gall bladder surgery. So she and 80-year-old Noah rented an adobe house in Arizona, near Tucson. Unable to keep up her usual pace, she wrote about her frustration to a friend: "All in God's name I want to do is work. It is infuriating to have to fight to be well enough to move about."

Margaret soon took up art classes, and she began to host lavish dinner parties. Both Grant and Stuart visited her on their vacations, and this pleased her very much. Noah grew weaker, both physically and emotionally.

Margaret began work on another autobiography, *Margaret Sanger: An Autobiography.*

Her work in birth control took on a new focus. She realized that the poorest women in the country, especially those in rural areas, were still untouched by the movement. To serve these women, Margaret changed her mind about the right to prescribe contraceptives. Realizing that many women would never be able to afford doctors, Margaret urged that nurses and other medical personnel be allowed to prescribe contraceptives.

In 1937 state health clinics in North Carolina began to offer birth control services. South Carolina, Georgia, Florida, Virginia, Mississippi, and Alabama followed suit. Staff in these clinics provided birth control information and devices, offered premarital counseling, helped to train doctors, and talked with couples about personal problems.

By the end of 1939, there were some 539 birth

control centers functioning in 42 states.

Margaret turned her attention to the poor of the Southwest. These families were suffering from the Great Depression and an especially long dry spell.

Margaret and her supporters took their information, diagrams, and devices to farm labor camps. Right from the start, the meetings were popular. The federal agencies in charge of these camps agreed to cooperate. Soon, 25 camps in California and Arizona offered birth control services.

In 1939 the American Birth Control League became the Birth Control Federation of America. Margaret was named honorary chairman. This new group included men among its leaders. Margaret and others thought that having males in the organization might attract more men in support of the cause.

However, the male leaders were not as aggressive as their female predecessors had been. They did not support Margaret when groups tried to prohibit her from speaking. They failed to support a referendum in Massachusetts challenging the law against birth control. When the Boston Public Library removed her autobiography, saying that it was obscene, the men did not protest.

Still, the Birth Control Federation of America met the needs of many women. Clinics served more than

16,000 patients and had contacts with 34,000 women. They charged as little as one cent and as much as one dollar. Some of their services were free.

Margaret was invited to sit on a presidential committee concerned with health and welfare. She told the group that 37 percent of the national income was spent on welfare, much of it to support unwanted children. This was one reason, she argued, why public funding of birth control should be accepted. Another reason focused on mothers and children: "It will probably do more for the health and happiness of mothers and children than any other single instrument."

On December 7, 1941, the Japanese Air Force bombed American ships at Pearl Harbor. The United States declared war on Japan. Margaret wrote in her journal that day: "Nation after nation will now join in this madness & God only can keep hearts true."

Despite the horrifying news, First Lady Eleanor Roosevelt kept a luncheon engagement with Margaret on the following day. Mrs. Roosevelt said: "It seems to be the almost unanimous opinion that the time is opportune for developing child-spacing programs." A child-spacing program would help women space out the births of their children, not limit family size. This was not the same focus as Margaret's goal of "every child a wanted child."

In 1942 leaders in the Birth Control Federation of America announced a major change in policy. They, too, would focus on child spacing. They changed the name of the organization to Planned Parenthood Federation of America (PPFA).

Meanwhile World War II intensified. The Allied powers—the United States, Great Britain, France, the Soviet Union, and some smaller countries—fought in the Atlantic and Pacific oceans and in Europe against the Axis powers—Germany, Japan, and Italy.

Because of the war, political leaders no longer supported birth control. In Germany, Nazi leaders encouraged men and women to increase the population. In Japan, birth control clinics were closed. In France, male babies were hailed as potential soldiers.

Support for birth control slowed throughout America, too. A court closed a mothers' clinic in Massachusetts. In Connecticut, a ban on the use of contraceptives was upheld. In Boston, a priest warned his parishioners: "Nations preaching birth control will disappear from the stage of life."

However, this attitude changed as American workers left their jobs to fight in the military. Women had to take the men's places in factories and offices. Pregnant women and those with young children could not easily substitute for the men. The United States

Public Health Service became active in family planning. The health service no longer refused to honor a state's request for funding for family planning. It actively promoted contraception.

The Catholic church maintained consistent opposition to birth control: "The practice of artificial birth control inevitably brings in its train woeful consequences to the individual, the family, the State and the Nation."

In the summer of 1942, Noah suffered a severe stroke. He became partially paralyzed. Margaret gave up all her work to be with him constantly. She took up painting to occupy her in times when Noah didn't need her. She even took a correspondence course in art.

Noah died in June of 1943. Margaret wrote, ". . . only the goodness, kindness and loving things remain in my thoughts of J. Noah. I'm glad of that."

Both Stuart and Grant were military doctors, serving overseas. Grant saw action in the Pacific; Stuart served in Europe. Margaret was fearful for both her sons. She wrote in her diary: "I've always said since Peggy's death that life could not hold me long if another of my children went before I do."

Both sons were safe in 1945, when the Axis surrendered to the Allies, ending the war.

Margaret enjoyed Christmas Day 1945 with Grant

Margaret with her namesake, granddaughter Margaret Sanger Marston

and his wife and two sons, and with Stuart and his wife and two daughters. Stuart's first child was named Margaret Sanger II.

Margaret did not forget her cause. She was part of an association that urged Planned Parenthood to sponsor research into simpler and cheaper methods of birth control. In 1946, she traveled to Europe to help organize family planning conferences in Sweden and England. She also helped to organize an international birth control committee. This committee later became the International Planned Parenthood Federation.

Margaret was nearly 70 years old in 1948-1949 when she built a house in Tucson. There, she spent quite a bit of time painting. She decorated a mural in her home for her grandchildren. Despite a heart attack just before she moved into her new home, she soon had a wide circle of friends. When she was hostess, she often treated guests to international cooking, including some of her favorite curries.

Margaret also liked to go out. Her engagement book shows that she once went to nine dinner parties in a row. She had time for music as well as painting. Besides acquiring a fine library of records, she took piano lessons. She also learned to drive a car. Neighbors became used to seeing her drive around the community wearing a broad-brimmed straw hat and white cotton gloves.

Margaret received an honorary doctorate of law degree from Smith College in 1949. She was cited as "one who with deep sympathy for the oppressed and disinherited, yet with a dispassionate and scientific approach, has made a conspicuous contribution to human welfare through her integrity, courage and social vision."

Shortly after her 70th birthday, Margaret had

another heart attack and was in the hospital for two months. She admitted in a letter to a friend that heart trouble frightened her: "Just one little beat too few, & out you go."

More and more, she used painkilling drugs that sometimes caused violent mood swings. She also tried to control her body through her mind. She enrolled in a mail-order course in self-realization. About this time, she assembled a collection of papers and letters that showed the history of her career. She planned to give them to the Smith College Library, in hopes that they might inspire others to accept a challenge as she had.

In 1949 she received an invitation from old friends in Japan, asking her to come back to help Japanese families. Japanese officials had legalized both sterilization and abortion to limit families. Margaret's friends wanted her to explain to the officials that contraception was a better way to limit families. For the second time, she was refused permission to enter Japan. This time the refusal came from an American. The Allies had appointed American General Douglas MacArthur as temporary ruler of the defeated country. MacArthur would not grant her permission, saying that his decision was "purely on a matter of principle." He did not say what this principle was.

Margaret had to be content with raising funds in the United States to support birth control clinics in Japan.

Friends placed her name in consideration for the Nobel Peace Prize. Although she did not win that award, she was awarded the famous Lasker Prize for pioneering work in family planning.

In April 1951, MacArthur was removed from his post. In October 1952, Margaret traveled to Japan, where a cheering crowd greeted her in Yokohama with a crown of yellow chrysanthemums. Everywhere she went, sound trucks announced her presence: "Sanger is here!"

She left Yokohama for Bombay, India, where she attended the International Planned Parenthood Federation Conference. At that meeting, Margaret was named an honorary president of the Family Planning Association in India.

Margaret experienced more health problems. In her daily journal, she wrote of both sickness and health. She exercised, explored diets that included yogurt, wheat germ, and honey, and took lots of vitamin E.

Despite the problems, Margaret traveled to Stockholm for an International Planned Parenthood Conference in 1953. There she was named president of the conference.

An admirer described the 74-year-old lady: "Pretty as a picture with a cartwheel hat on a head of soft curls and the most sincere and dear face one could imagine." Participants called her an "international citizen." In a speech, she said: "I believed it was my duty to place motherhood on a higher level than enslavement and accident. For these beliefs I was denounced, arrested, I was in and out of police courts and higher courts, indictments hung over my life for several years. But nothing could alter my beliefs."

The next year she traveled to Japan to take part in the first national meeting of the Japan Federation of Family Planning.

Margaret was thrilled at the news of a safe and effective birth control pill in 1956.

In that same year, her journal entries again tell of illness:

Sept 27 pain all day
Sept 29 difficult breathing
Nov 18 pain left shoulder, just spreading pain
Dec 28 hospital again for thyroid test

She did give talks occasionally, but she did not regain her energy, optimism, and cheerfulness. She suffered from chest pains. Open-heart surgery was considered, but doctors believed it was too risky for a woman of Margaret's age and condition.

In 1958, Margaret sent New Year's greetings to friends and supporters. "I survey the progress our movement has made around the world and find much to praise. Nations are making birth control devices part of their national policy, and of their public health and welfare programs."

With the help of a traveling companion, she made the trip to New Delhi, India, for the Sixth International Conference on Planned Parenthood in 1959. At that meeting, Dr. Gregory Pincus, one of the inventors of the birth control pill, dedicated his research to Margaret.

She was so weak that she used a wheelchair when she returned to the United States. However, in a few months, she could not resist making another trip to Japan. The Japanese were celebrating the fact that they had cut their birth rate in half in less than ten years. They honored Margaret with a key to their capital city of Tokyo.

The next year, she criticized President Dwight Eisenhower for not including family planning in his programs of aid to other countries. The 80-year-old Sanger challenged the president to a debate, saying he needed to be "straightened out." Eisenhower refused the challenge.

When Catholic John F. Kennedy was nominated for president in 1960, the Emotional Margaret declared that she would leave the country if he were elected. She believed that a Catholic president would bring back the birth control restrictions she had fought against for 50 years.

When Kennedy was elected, the Thinking Margaret changed her mind. She would give him a year's trial, she said, before she moved out of the country. She was glad she waited. One of Kennedy's first moves as president was to accept the Draper Report, which advocated giving birth control information to any nation that asked for it.

By 1965, Margaret's heart problems had weakened her greatly. She was confined first to a bed at home and then to a nursing home. On good days, when her mind was clear, Margaret talked with visitors. Some days she sat up in bed to read and reread the mail that still came to her in a steady stream. She became more and more tired mentally and physically. Her mind wandered often, usually into the past.

On September 6, 1966, 87-year-old Margaret Sanger died.

In an obituary, the *New York Times* called her "one of history's great rebels and a monumental figure of the first half of the twentieth century."

This "monumental figure" had once been a child who almost lost her life to conquer her fear of a railroad bridge. She was a daughter who watched her mother die from tuberculosis made worse by pregnancies. She was a nurse who watched women lose their physical and emotional health as their families grew too large to handle. She was a lover of children who believed that every child should be a wanted child. She was a student, a researcher, and a public speaker. She was a woman who was scorned, humiliated, arrested, and jailed.

Margaret was almost alone when she began her fight to make birth control both acceptable and available. The people who opposed her views are too many to name: federal, state, and local officials; members of the medical profession; church leaders and members; liberal reformers; conservatives; the press; men and women of every economic class and social level.

What did she accomplish?

Millions of young men and women now speak about sex as a normal part of their lives. Millions of husbands and wives now accept the responsibility of planning their families. Millions of women now accept the challenge of controlling their own bodies. Millions of us are inspired to fight for what we believe in, to leave the world better because we have dwelt in it.

Appendix One
A Glossary of Special Terms

abortion: termination of pregnancy before a fetus is fully developed

American Birth Control League: a lobby group created by Margaret Sanger to promote birth control clinics and legislation

birth control: regulation of conception

Birth Control Clinical Research Bureau: an organization established by Margaret Sanger in 1923 to provide birth control services and to conduct research on family planning

Birth Control Federation of America: a combined organization of the American Birth Control League and other birth control supporters established in 1939

Birth Control Review: a publication, begun by Margaret Sanger and Frederick Blossom, that advocated birth control. The first issue appeared in 1917.

birth control pill: an oral contraceptive first available to the American public in the early 1960s

Brownsville Clinic: first birth control clinic in the United States, opened by Margaret Sanger in Brooklyn, New York, 1916

Call: a New York Socialist daily paper, which printed articles by Margaret Sanger

child spacing: concept that women should not have babies less than two years apart

Comstock Laws: laws put into effect in 1873 that outlawed mailing of materials considered "obscene," "lewd," and "lascivious"

condom: a sheath that covers the penis during sexual intercourse to protect against venereal disease and conception

contraception: prevention of conception

diaphragm: a flexible disk that covers the uterine cervix and thus prevents conception during intercourse *eugenics:* the study of human improvement that advocates restricting the right to be a parent to those people judged emotionally and physically "fit."

National Birth Control League: an organization established in 1915 to reform federal and state Comstock Laws

pessary: a device similar to a diaphragm

Planned Parenthood Federation of America: a union of the Birth Control Federation of America and supporters of child spacing in 1942

pregnancy: period when a developing fetus is carried in the uterus

rhythm: a method of birth control in which the woman avoids intercourse during the days of the month during which she is ovulating

sanatorium: a hospital for the treatment of infectious diseases like tuberculosis

Socialist: a person who believes that the government should control most business and property

sperm: the male reproductive cell

sponge: a device that absorbs liquids. Sponges soaked with spermicide are sometimes used for contraception.

suppository: a device inserted into the vagina to create a chemical change to prevent conception

tuberculosis: an infectious disease that attacks many parts of the body, especially the lungs

venereal disease: a contagious disease contracted through sexual intercourse

The Woman Rebel: a monthly newspaper begun by Margaret Sanger in 1914 to educate women and to challenge the Comstock Laws

Appendix Two
Margaret Sanger: A Time Line

1879–Margaret Louisa Higgins is born.

1899–Enrolls in three-year nurse's training course.

1902–Marries Bill Sanger.

1903–Stuart Sanger is born.

1908–Grant Sanger is born.

1910–Peggy Sanger is born.

1912–Begins work as childbirth nurse in tenements.

1912-1913–Writes "What Every Girl Should Know" column for the *Call*.

1913–"What Every Girl Should Know" is banned by postal authorities.

1914–Publishes the *Woman Rebel*.

1914–Arrested for indecent articles and for using the mail to "incite murder and assassination."

1914–Writes *Family Limitation*.

1915–Peggy dies.

1916–Case against her (for charges made in 1914) is dismissed.

1916–Arrested for selling *Family Limitation*; is freed.

1916–Publishes first copies of *Birth Control Review*.

1916–Opens Brownsville Clinic.

1916–Is arrested when Brownsville Clinic is raided by police.

1917–Sentenced to 30 days in prison.

1920–Publishes *Woman and the New Race*.

1921–Divorces Bill Sanger.

1921–Arrested at Town Hall meeting; case is dismissed.

1922–Marries J. Noah Slee.

1923–Opens Birth Control Clinical Research Bureau.

1926–Publishes *Happiness in Marriage*.

1927–Helps organize World Population conference in Geneva.

1931–Organizes National Committee on Federal Legislation for Birth Control.

1930-1936–Lobbies in Congress for legislation to support acceptance of birth control.

1943–J. Noah Slee dies.

1943-1966–Works for cause despite failing health.

1966–Margaret Higgins Sanger dies.

Selected Bibliography

Calder, Jenni. *Women and Marriage in Victorian Fiction.* New York: Oxford University Press, 1976

Chesler, Ellen. *Margaret Sanger: Woman of Valor.* New York: Simon & Schuster, 1992

Dimitroff, Thomas and Lois Janes, eds. *Andaste Inquirer.* Corning: Corning-Painted Post Historical Society, 1978

Douglas, Emily Taft. *Margaret Sanger: Pioneer of the Future.* New York: Holt, Rinehart and Winston, 1970

Gordon, Linda. *Woman's Body, Woman's Right.* New York: Grossman, 1976

Gray, Madeline. *Margaret Sanger.* New York: Richard Marek, 1979

Kennedy, David M. *Birth Control in America.* New Haven: Yale University Press, 1970

Lader, Lawrence. *The Margaret Sanger Story.* New York: Doubleday, 1955

Lader, Lawrence and Milton Meltzer. *Margaret Sanger: Pioneer of Birth Control.* New York: Thomas Y. Crowell, 1969

Library of Congress. *Margaret Sanger: A Register of Her Papers in the Library of Congress.* Washington: Library of Congress, 1977

Reed, James. *From Private Vice to Public Virtue.* New York: Basic Books, 1978

Sanger, Margaret. *My Fight for Birth Control.* New York: Farrar & Rinehart, 1931

———. *Margaret Sanger: An Autobiography.* New York: W. Norton & Co., 1938

———. *Motherhood in Bondage.* New York: Maxwell Reprint Co., 1928

———. *Woman and the New Race.* New York: Maxwell Reprint Co., 1920.

Scott, Anne Firor. *Making the Invisible Woman Visible.* Chicago: University of Illinois Press, 1984

Sophia Smith Collection. Northampton, Mass.: assorted photos, letters, messages, mementos

Author's Note

Margaret Sanger wrote two autobiographies and several other books. She wrote with charm, style, and drama. Several Sanger biographers used these books as basic sources of information. Recently, other biographers have searched extensively through reports, letters, notes, and other primary sources. These later biographers have questioned, modified, and sometimes contradicted some of the information in Sanger's work. In *Margaret Sanger: "Every Child a Wanted Child,"* I have used primary sources wherever possible.

Index

abortion, 37, 39, 40, 50, 56, 81, 91, 134, 147
American Birth Control League, 111, 123, 124, 141
American Medical Association, 116
anarchists, 33
Anthony, Susan B., 14
Astor, John Jacob, 32

birth control, 9, 33, 34, 36-39, 43-45, 47, 48, 50, 51, 52, 53, 56, 58, 59, 61, 65, 66, 69-71, 73, 75, 77, 83, 84, 86-88, 92, 93, 95, 98-100, 102, 108, 109, 110, 112-115, 118-120, 124, 127, 128, 130, 131, 133-135, 140-145, 147, 150, 151, 152
Birth Control (film), 91, 93
Birth Control Clinical Research Bureau, 113, 114, 117, 123, 125, 127-130
Birth Control Federation of America, 141, 143
birth control pill, 149, 150
Birth Control Review, 70, 84, 88, 89, 91-93, 115-116, 124
Blackwell's Island (Roosevelt Island), 78, 79, 84
Blossom, Frederick, 70, 88, 89, 91, 92
Bocker, Dr. Dorothy, 112, 113, 115
Brooklyn Daily Eagle, 74
Brownsville Clinic, 71, 73, 74, 75, 76, 82, 91, 127
Byrne, Ethel, 71, 73, 76, 77, 78, 79, 81, 82, 85, 90, 100

Call, 38, 39, 41, 42
Canada, 54, 119
Capitalists, 33, 43, 50
child-spacing programs, 142, 143
China, 109, 110
church attitudes on birth control, 48, 51, 66, 93, 105, 106, 131, 143, 144, 152
Claverack College, 16, 17, 19, 65
Committee of 100, 77, 81, 85, 86
Communists, 33
Comstock, Anthony, 37, 48
Comstock Laws (obscenity laws), 37, 42, 45, 47, 48, 63, 69, 98
Corning, New York, 7, 11, 15, 20
Curly, Mayor James Michael, 124

Dennett, Mary Ware, 59, 61, 77
Dickinson, Dr. Robert, 59, 115
Draper Report, 151
"Dutch Methods of Birth Control," 59

Einstein, Albert, 108
Eisenhower, Dwight, 150
Ellis, Havelock, 57

England, 53, 54, 55, 56, 58, 99, 118, 145
Ernst, Morris, 127, 128, 135, 136
eugenicists, 33, 108
Europe, 45, 99, 114, 123, 144, 145
"Every child a wanted child", 42, 134, 142

Family Limitation, 52, 53, 54, 60, 68, 86, 110, 112
feminists, 43-44, 63
First American Birth Control Conference, 102

Geneva, Switzerland, 121
Germany, 91, 92, 99, 100, 143
Goldman, Emma, 33, 34
Goldstein, Jonah J., 76, 77, 84, 87, 90, 95
Great Depression, 133, 134, 141

Halpern, Rose, 77
Halton, Dr. Mary, 70-71
Happiness in Marriage, 120
Hastings-on-Hudson, New York, 29, 45, 47
Hayes, Archbishop Patrick J., 104, 105
Higgins, Michael, 12, 13, 14, 15, 20, 31, 32, 33, 44
Higgins, Anne, 13, 14, 15, 20, 27, 152
Higgins, Nan, 25
Holland, 53, 58
Hoover, Herbert, 133

"In Defense of Assassination," 51
infanticide, 56, 57
International Birth Control Conference, 116, 117
International Medical Group, 135
International Planned Parenthood Federation, 146, 148
International Union for the Scientific Investigation of Population, 123

Japan, 108-110, 142, 143, 147, 148, 149, 150
Japan Federation of Family Planning, 149

Kennedy, John F., 151

Lasker Prize for pioneering work in family planning, 148
League of Nations, 121
Lewis, Corrections Commissioner Burdette, 79, 82

MacArthur, General Douglas, 147, 148
Mallett, Sir Bernard, 122
Malthus, Thomas, 57
Margaret Sanger: An Autobiography, 140
Massachusetts, 44, 74, 141, 143
McCann, Joseph, 88, 90

Medical Journal and Record, 118
Mindell, Fania, 73, 74, 75, 76, 82, 86, 95
Moore, Hazel, 134
Motherhood in Bondage, 123
My Fight for Birth Control, 132

National Birth Control League, 59, 61, 76, 108
National Committee on Federal Legislation for Birth Control (NCFLBC), 130, 131, 136, 137
New Woman's Society of Japan, 109
New York Academy of Medicine, 59, 61, 127, 128, 131
New York Birth Control League, 70
New York County Medical Society, 127
New York Herald Tribune, 128, 132
New York Times, 73, 77, 79, 83, 120, 151
New York Tribune, 82

Paris, France, 45, 47
Pincus, Dr. Gregory, 150
Pivot of Civilization, The, 107, 108
Place, Francis, 57
Planned Parenthood Federation of America (PPFA), 143, 145
Pope Pius XI, 131
Practices of Contraception, 135
President's Committee on Social Trends, 131
"Prevention of Conception, The," 50
Prohibition, 114, 133
Psychology of Sex, 57

Raymond Street Jail, 75, 76
Rhythm, 135
Riis, Jacob, 32
Roosevelt, Eleanor, 133, 142
Roosevelt, Franklin, 133
Roosevelt, Theodore, 67, 84, 93
Russell, Bertrand, 108

St. Louis City Men's Club, 67
Sanger, Bill, 24-33, 36, 45, 47, 53, 55, 56, 58-60, 69, 77, 91, 99-101
Sanger, Grant, 31, 53, 61, 91, 98, 100, 109, 110, 120, 123, 131, 132, 140, 144, 145
Sanger, Margaret (Maggie Louisa Higgins):
  arrests of, 33, 51, 61, 68, 69, 74, 75, 76, 104, 105, 109
  as an artist, 140, 144, 146
  autobiographies of, 19, 39, 62, 102, 132, 140, 141
  birth of, 9, 11
  as a child, 7, 8, 11, 12, 14, 15, 16
  conquering fears, 7-9, 12, 19, 38, 65, 66, 102, 103, 121, 152
  death of, 151
  education of, 16, 17, 19
  ill health of, 22, 27, 28, 98, 100, 139, 140, 146, 147, 148, 149, 150, 151
  marriage and, 20, 24, 25, 26, 58, 101, 102, 110, 111, 133, 134
  as a mother, 28, 29, 31, 53, 55, 56, 60, 61, 62, 91, 98, 100, 123, 125, 126, 132, 144
  as a nurse, 20, 22, 24, 25, 26, 31, 34, 39, 152
  as a teacher, 20
  trials of, 53, 54, 61, 62, 63, 76, 77, 78, 82, 87, 135
Sanger, Margaret II, 145
Sanger, Peggy, 31, 53, 54, 55, 56, 60, 61, 62, 144
Sanger, Stuart, 28, 29, 53, 55, 61, 91, 98, 100, 120, 123, 125, 126, 140, 144, 145
Schlesinger, Arthur Sr., 125
Section 1142 of the Penal Code, 75, 76, 77-78, 83, 85, 86, 127
Section 1145 of the Penal Code, 69, 70, 95
Silecchia, Vito, 114
Sixth International Conference on Planned Parenthood, 150
Slee, J. Noah, 101, 102, 109-111, 114, 118-122, 130, 133, 134, 139, 140, 144
Smith College, 146, 147, 157
Socialists, 13, 33, 38, 44, 52, 77, 101
Stone, Dr. Hannah, 115, 117, 134-136

Tucson, Arizona, 139, 146

United States Public Health Service, 143-144

Voluntary Parenthood League, 108

Wells, H. G., 99, 108
"What Every Girl Should Know," 41, 42, 73, 76, 82, 94
Whitman, Governor Charles S., 81, 85
Willowlake, 111, 120
Wilson, Woodrow, 91
Woman and the New Race, 98, 99, 107
Woman Rebel, 47, 48, 49, 50, 51, 89
World, 105
World War I, 53, 87, 91-93, 97, 98, 100
World War II, 142, 143, 144

Yale University, 98, 120